The author did all his writing in a morris chair with a wide lapboard before him. All he needed was plenty of paper and sharpened pencils. His imagination and amazing memory did the rest.

NE GREY

MAN OF THE WEST

by JEAN KARR, 1906 -

New York

GREENBERG : PUBLISHER

ZANE GREY

By

W. Livingston Larned

Been to Avalon with Grey . . . been most everywhere;
Chummed with him and fished with him in every Sports-
man's lair.
Helped him with the white Sea-bass and Barracuda haul,
Shared the Tuna's sprayful sport and heard his Hunter-
call,
Me an' Grey are fishin' friends . . . Pals of rod and reel,
Whether it's the sort that fights . . . or th' humble eel,
On and on, through Wonderland . . . winds a-blowin' free,
Catching all th' fins that grow . . . Sportsman Grey an' Me.

Been to Florida with Zane . . . scouting down th' coast;
Whipped the deep for Tarpon, too, that natives love th'
most.
Seen the smiling, tropic isles that pass, in green review,
Gathered cocoanut and moss where Southern skies were blue.
Seen him laugh that boyish laugh, when things were goin'
right;
Helped him beach our little boat and kindle fires at night.
Comrades of the Open Way, the Treasure-Trove of Sea,
Port Ahoy and who cares where, with Mister Grey an' Me!

Been to Western lands with Grey . . . hunted fox and deer.
Seen the Grizzly's ugly face with danger lurkin' near.

iii

Slept on needles, near th' sky, and marked th' round moon
  rise
Over purpling peaks of snow that hurt a fellow's eyes.
Gone, like Indians, under brush and to some mystic place—
Home of red men, long since gone, to join their dying race.
Yes . . . we've chummed it, onward—outward . . . moun-
  tain, wood, and key,
At the quiet readin'-table . . . Sportsman Grey an' Me.

From *Tales of Fishes,*
Harper & Brothers, 1919.

Contents

Acknowledgments

Among individuals who lent their assistance to the author the following deserve special thanks: Mr. Norris Schneider, teacher and Zanesville (Ohio) historian; and Mr. Ed McCaddon, sole survivor of Zane Grey's boyhood "Terrace Gang."

For background information I am indebted to Harper and Brothers; to the staff of Grosset and Dunlap, particularly to Mr. Hugh Juergens for his splendid co-operation; to Mr. Benjamin Rudd of the Library of Congress; and to Mrs. Lola Bikul for her valuable suggestions and advice; also to Miss Nellie K. Ball and Mr. George M. Cohen for their assistance in preparing the manuscript.

Too numerous to mention are the many older residents of Zanesville who contributed a wealth of personal anecdotes gleaned from their recollections of Zane Grey as a boy.

JEAN KARR

Washington, D.C.

List of Illustrations

Preface

"Mr. Grey, what would you say is the secret of your success?"

It was the old question. He had heard it a thousand times, from baffled critics, admiring readers, inquiring reporters, and aspiring young writers. He had always managed *an* answer, but never *the* answer. "Hard work and perseverance," he might say on one occasion. Another time the substance of his reply would be "Sincerity," or still another, "The faith of my wife in my ability to succeed."

Zane Grey was aware that his answers were inadequate, for the question—natural as it is, and simple as it may sound—is a complex one, calling for more insight and objectivity than any writer can be expected to have in a discussion of himself or his works. Even the critics, whose business it is to explain these things, are usually incapable of wholly satisfactory explanations. This was especially true in the case of Zane Grey, whose rapid rise to best-seller fame was nothing short of phenomenal.

Here was a man who, with no special training in writing, with nothing to sustain him except his belief in himself, abandoned a profession which would at least have afforded a decent living for his family and himself, and in the most miserable poverty doggedly persisted toward

ix

his goal of becoming an author. To make the puzzle more baffling, his works were repeatedly rejected by astute publishers who were convinced that the man had no talent whatsoever, either for fiction or non-fiction, and that his works would never sell.

For years the determined author financed himself or relied on the generosity of his family while he experimented with all kinds of writing, even publishing some at his own expense. He was thirty-five years old, and had accumulated a staggering collection of rejections, before a publisher accepted one of his novels. This, it must be noted, was done with some misgiving and with no assurance that the author's future manuscripts would be given favorable consideration.

Twenty years later, skeptical publishers were still marveling at Zane Grey's mounting success. A total of twenty-five novels had sold during that period over seventeen million copies to an enthusiastic reading public estimated at 56 million. Demand for reprint rights and movie rights was almost taken for granted. Foreign editions had appeared in twenty different languages, including French, Spanish, German, Italian, and the Scandinavian. In 1948, nine years after the death of Zane Grey, his books were still in constant demand and his publishers reported a total sale of 28 million copies of his sixty-nine titles.

It read like a Horatio Alger success story. It was too fantastic to be believed.

Yet all the while, critics were insisting that this author, who had won himself a permanent place in the hearts of his readers with his dashing tales of American frontier life and the glamorous West, really had no talent for writing at all. They said he lacked humor and fluency. Some said his plots were improbable, his views of life unrealistic. Others said his characterization lacked "subtlety" and "finesse." As for his style, some labeled it "tedious" and others said it was "archaic" and "stiff." His publishers termed it "bludgy," a word of doubtful meaning which exists, if at all, only in the secret dictionary of publishers; but though its definition is not clear, its very sound implies unfavorable criticism. Burton Rascoe was even less kindly but far more specific on the subject of style when he stated flatly that Zane Grey possessed no merit whatsoever, "in either style or substance."

But still his stories sold, in book form and as magazine serials; reprint sales were assured; Hollywood producers clamored for movie rights. This despite all the qualities in which, according to the critics, Zane Grey was lacking. Where, then, was the answer?

"Luck!" chorused the critics, hastening to explain that the West was still new and exciting—a place of escape for office-weary Easterners and a source of pride to native Westerners. The writer had simply been fortunate in hitting upon a background that caught the public fancy. Luckily, too, his travels through the American Southwest had served to lend authenticity to his descriptions and local color.

Having summed up the success secret in one syllable, the critics relaxed, smugly unaware of the flaw in their reasoning that had produced, again, only a partial explanation.

Of course there was an element of luck in Zane Grey's success, as in the success of any writer. Zane Grey would have been the last to deny it and the first to acknowledge its weight. Having suffered ill fortune for so many years, he was all the more impressed by the unpredictable change in his luck. For he knew only too well that the success or failure of a book may depend on the timeliness of its subject; on an editor's mood, on the relative merits of other manuscripts currently competing for the publisher's attention; on the temper of the people and the manner in which a book is presented to them. It would have been foolish to ignore the importance of luck, but it would have been infinitely more foolish to rely upon luck alone.

Further disproving the claims of the critics who attributed his success to the fortunate choice of the Western theme was the evidence of Grey's increasing popularity in other fields. His Western romances had undoubtedly earned his reputation, but not all his works were of the West, and yet they sold. As time went by, there was more and more demand for the historical novels he had written early in his career, and at the same time he was earning a reputation as the writer of books for boys, stories of college days, of baseball and the world of sports, of outdoor adventures in hunting and fishing.

That presented another phase of the puzzle: the variety in his topics and the variety in the types of people who read his books. He had a faithful audience among office workers, cab drivers, miners, sportsmen, factory workers and professional men, newsboys and millionaires. His public included women as well as men: secretaries, salesgirls, schoolteachers, and housewives. Moreover, his popularity had spread all over the country, East and West, North and South, though publishers' figures revealed the inexplicable fact that sales percentages were highest in New York and Boston.

Then, for a time, it became the vogue among critics to interpret everything in the light of the American spirit, a newly-discovered, intangible something that fed upon national heritage. Literary circles began to recognize the merit of folk-lore and legend, of ballads and anecdotes that had sprung up spontaneously as a part of

American growth. Mythical figures took their places along with national heroes in the formation of the cultural pattern. Paul Bunyan and his Blue Ox were as American as George Washington and the cherry tree, and "Casey Jones" was as American as "The Star-Spangled Banner." Possibly Zane Grey had his place in the establishment of "the great American epic."

Here the critics were hitting closer to the mark, for without doubt Zane Grey's themes were thoroughly American, dealing with the rigors of frontier life and the heroic characters it produced; Indian massacres and the American Revolution; the vastness and promise of the West; the appeal of outdoor life; hunting and fishing; riding and roping; school days and baseball, the national sport. Naturally Americans liked to read of the exploits of their pioneer forebears, of the wealth in resources and opportunity their country offered, of their favorite sports and their fondest memories.

But the Zane Grey appeal was more than national; it was universal. Millions of copies of his books, in English and in translation, were sold on the European continent, in South America, Africa, and Australia. Several queens of Europe listed him among their favorite writers. The Queen of Rumania so admired his books that she requested him to dedicate one to her. In Paris his books were among the most popular "Foreign Fiction." In a Spanish castle, an American visitor observed shelf upon shelf of books bound in immaculate white leather, while on the table lay a leather volume, well-worn and soiled, bearing the familiar title, *Riders of the Purple Sage*. Apparently the field of Americana was being discovered abroad as well as at home—but surely there was something to explain why Zane Grey's own particular contribution to Americana found such favor abroad.

Failing to find the answer to their question either in a study of Zane Grey's writings or of his readers, critics were at last prompted to take a closer look at the man himself. It was a good idea, but like many a good idea, it was not entirely successful.

They were impressed by the man's quiet manner, his rugged features, his appearance of indefatigability. He was not the powerful giant that people were inclined to picture when they read of his adventurous life; rather, he was surprisingly slight of build, with a wiriness that suggested great physical stamina supplemented by a kind of restless nervous energy. In countenance and dress he looked the part of the outdoorsman. His face, heavily bronzed by wind and sun, looked more youthful than the contrasting thatch of grey hair. His bright eyes were keenly observing, and yet at the same time gave the impression of looking far into the distance. His expression was usually grave and intent, but his smile was quick and friendly.

He created the impression of a man who has lived an active and interesting life, but disappointingly enough, he did not give the appearance of a successful writer, much less a world-known celebrity. He was quiet, reserved, almost shy. His extreme reluctance to talk about himself or his private life made interviewers acutely aware of the difficulty of their assignment, but equally aware that the object of their study was not being deliberately uncommunicative. In fact, he was half-apologetic about his conversational shortcomings and would occasionally confess, with a self-conscious smile, "I was never much good at talking."

On some topics he spoke easily and enthusiastically— baseball, fishing, hunting, photography, his family—but about himself he had little to say. At the close of an interview, interrogators would realize that they still knew practically nothing of Zane Grey, the man.

The curious and significant fact was that *Zane Grey's readers knew him*—his character, his personality, his ambitions and ideals, his moral code and his basic philosophy. Through his writings he revealed himself to the sympathetic reader, although it is quite possible that the critic's eye, unaided by the light of sympathy, could never have seen the invisible man behind the closely-packed lines of narrative. Like the elves and brownies who are visible only to the eyes of believing children, Zane Grey was visible only to those who shared the same daydreams and hopes, the same love of natural beauty and craving for adventure.

Sympathy unites kindred spirits, and Zane Grey's readers were quick to recognize his sympathetic interest in them. If, as the critics said, his style was labored and lacking in fluency, that was all to the good, for it identified him among his readers, not as a professional writer with a glib pen and a ready stock of high-flown phrases, but as an ordinary man like themselves, struggling to understand his own reactions, struggling to express his innermost feelings, and half-shy in doing so. They knew, from newspaper accounts, that he no longer lived in poverty or in the boredom of office routine, yet his success and freedom never instilled envy in their hearts, for he had not lost the common touch. They knew his humble gratitude for the life that was his, and his compassion for the less fortunate with whom he was always eager to share the benefits of his experiences. They felt his imaginative sympathy kindle as he watched the laborers in the Death Valley borax mines, surrounded by a cloud of choking dust, day in, day out, deprived of the clean fresh air, the open spaces, the smell of the salt sea, because "love, or duty, or economic necessity" bound them to their work. They never begrudged him his comfortable homes, his private yacht which with its fishing gear was said to have cost a million dollars. That was his realm and he deserved it; but the wonderful part about it was that he was living for them the adventures they could not have themselves. He had done what all men long to do: he had made his wildest daydreams become realities.

Zane Grey became a friend to his readers. They liked him for his simple tastes, his devotion to his home and family, his genuine love of nature, his ideals of sportsmanship and his code of chivalry. They respected him for his religious beliefs, simple, sincere, and unfaltering. They liked him because he was generous and tolerant, quite positive in his likes and dislikes, and outspoken in expressing them. They admired his rough, rugged cowboys who, though lacking the veneer of convention, could be relied upon to conduct themselves as gentlemen.

Zane Grey was criticized for not producing realism in an age when realism was the literary vogue, and fellow-writers had gone overboard for Freudian psychology. But the success of his romances—clean as an ocean breeze —proved that thousands of people, like himself, were revolted by the crudeness and vulgarity of modern fiction; that they liked to think, as he did, that men are essentially decent and can rise to untold heights of nobility, given half a chance.

No one would deny that he presented a glamorized version of life, but the truth of the matter is, he wrote about life as he lived it and saw it. Instinctively he sought beauty, purity, and simplicity of life. He was repelled by the sordid and ugly. He was not blind to its existence, but his awareness of it enhanced his appreciation of the better things: the eternal beauty of age-old mountains, the mystic loneliness of the desert, the ever-changing colors of the skies, the sweeping freshness of the ocean, the fragrance of forests, and the fascination of all the creatures, great and small, that were a part of Nature's plan. Possibly it was a matter of luck that his everyday life was filled with glamor. But Nature had equipped him with rose-colored glasses, and he never outgrew his wonder at the world's treasures.

This was the world he wrote about. And as he wrote, he was constantly striving for a better understanding of himself and the people around him. To the many readers who already know him through his works, this story of his life is offered in the hope that it will bring a deeper understanding of Zane Grey, the man.

JEAN KARR,

Washington, D. C.

Zane Grey
MAN OF THE WEST

Jim of the Cave

Dr. Lewis Grey and his family lived on Convers Avenue in a section of Zanesville known as The Terrace. Behind the Grey home was an orchard and beyond the orchard was a dense thicket which provided an excellent hiding-place for a gang of young mischief-makers led by the oldest Grey boy.

Under his supervision, the youthful ruffians had dug a cave in the midst of the thicket. The location of the cave—indeed its very existence—was a deep secret. The digging had been accomplished mainly after dark, or, when daytime labor was necessary, under the watchful eyes of lookouts who gave warning if outsiders approached. Not even a handful of loose dirt was left to disclose the secret hiding-place. All the dirt displaced by excavation had been carefully packed into gunny sacks and carried away to be dumped at a safe distance from the cave.

The completion of the project was marked by a ceremony of dedication. With all the formalities of blood-letting and solemn oaths, the members of the gang adopted a set of by-laws, pledged loyalty to one another, and

I

swore to keep secret their organization and their meeting place.

Then they turned to the task of interior decorating. A board partition was erected to divide the cave into two rooms, the first being a spacious lobby which led in turn to the inner sanctum. The bookshelf held the place of honor with a complete collection of "Beadle's Dime Library" and the novels of Harry Castlemon. Only through a deed of great daring or courage could a member earn the privilege of reading one of these tattered volumes.

The walls of the cave were covered with pictures and hung with crude weapons, hand-made. A stone fireplace was built and around it was arranged an array of cooking utensils appropriated from various kitchens in the neighborhood. One family unwittingly contributed a kerosene lamp which provided a flickering light.

The lamp was smoky and the fireplace didn't draw properly, but the dim lamplight only added to the atmosphere of mystery and secrecy; and the fireplace could always be induced to give out enough heat to stew a "borrowed" chicken in a "borrowed" pot, or to roast potatoes filched from a neighboring garden.

Gradually the cave acquired makeshift beds of straw, old rugs and blankets and burlap bags, and the gang was ready to realize dreams of holding a secret all-night session. Elaborate plans were made in advance. Gardens, kitchens, and hen-roosts were pillaged for provender. Each boy told his parents he was invited to spend the night at another boy's home.

The plot was successful. One by one, the members of the secret order appeared at the hidden entrance, gave the password, and were admitted to the inner sanctum where the accumulated plunder was portioned out.

There was little more than a pretense of sleeping that

night. The high-light of the session was the reading of a manuscript titled "Jim of the Cave," a highly fictionalized narrative of a martyred gang, a secret cave, daring adventure and sudden death. The hero, Jim, lost his life, as did all his comrades, in defense of a lovely maiden with blue eyes and flaxen hair.

The manuscript had been written on the backs of strips of wallpaper, under conditions as discouraging to a young author as the proverbial dusty attic and crust of bread. He had toiled over it persistently, despite the distractions of whispered conversations among his plotting fellows, the suffocating fumes from the fireplace, and the wavering light from the kerosene lamp.

But at last it was finished, and on this special occasion it was read aloud. If the voice of the young reader choked and cracked from time to time, and if the eyes of his listeners blurred with tears, it probably was more from the smoking fireplace than from the excitement of the tale. Nevertheless, the story held the audience spellbound and they took pride in the portrayal of their gang as a group of "misunderstood boys" performing great feats of daring and gallantry. Most impressed of all was Jim, who was cast in the title role.

In real life, the Jim of the story became not a martyr, but a traitor. Not long after the all-night session, Jim was accused of breaking one of the sacred laws. He was tried and found guilty. The severity of the punishment was unprecedented in the gang's history: Jim was declared suspended until further notice.

Jim accepted his sentence silently and disappeared from the hideout. But he kept constant vigil from a hiding-place in the thicket near the mouth of the cave and awaited his opportunity for revenge. His chance came one night when the desperadoes raided a chicken-coop and all gathered around for the feast. In the midst of the revelry, Traitor Jim appeared at the entrance of the cave, leading with him the irate owner of the property on which the cave was located.

Dr. Grey ordered the culprits to forfeit all stolen properties, remove the roof of the cave, and fill up the hole. Special punishment was meted out to his own son, the ringleader of the gang and author of the wallpaper manuscript. Young Grey was whipped with a piece of Brussels carpet found on the floor of the cave. As for the manuscript, which might in future years have achieved untold value, it went up in smoke by order of the stern parent. And so the world will never see a compilation of The Complete Works of Zane Grey.

Years later, the author wrote the sequel to the cave episode in an article published by *The American Magazine:* "What I did to Jim, the Judas of our clan, was similar in part to the story he had inspired! In real life he grew up, passed me by with a stony stare, and married the light-haired girl."

The Terror of the Terrace

Zane Grey was fourteen years old at the time of the cave episode and the destruction of his first manuscript. He was born January 31, 1875, in the house on Convers Avenue. He had a sister, Ida, and two brothers, Cedar and Romer. The latter was called "Reddy" as a boy, but in later narratives of their hunting and fishing expeditions together, Grey referred to him invariably as "R.C."

The stern father who burned the precious manuscript of "Jim of the Cave" was well known in Zanesville as "Doc" Grey. He had taken up dentistry late in life after spending his earlier years as a backwoodsman, hunter, farmer, and preacher. He was apparently not too happy with his profession, for he loved the freedom of the outdoors, a love that his sons inherited.

The Grey ancestors were Irish immigrants who had settled first in Pennsylvania, moving later to Ohio. On the maternal side of the house was an even stronger tradition of adventurous living and the pioneer spirit, for Mrs. Grey was the former Alice Josephine Zane, one of the historic Zane family and a direct descendant of Colonel Ebenezer Zane who, exiled from his native Denmark,

5

shipped to America with William Penn. It was Colonel Zane who defended Fort Henry during siege after siege, conceived the idea of building a road through the wilderness in order to open up the Ohio River Valley for settlement, and, when the road was finished, received a land grant from Congress, including the part of Ohio that became the site of Zanesville. Through Colonel Zane's wife the Zanes were supposed to have acquired a trace of Indian blood, of which their descendants, the Grey boys in particular, were extremely proud.

For reasons best known to themselves, Doc Grey and his wife christened their oldest son Pearl. Possibly they had hoped for a girl; possibly the name of "Pearl Grey" afforded them some whimsical amusement. Or again, it may have been handed down as a family name. No one seems to know. Whatever the story underlying it, needless to say the name proved a handicap in many respects and produced its affect on the boy.

It was not until after the publication of his first book that he changed his name to "Zane," in honor of his maternal ancestors. He had been embarrassed by the volume of his fan mail addressed, naturally, to "Miss Pearl Grey," and the final decision to abandon his given name came when he overheard two young women on a train discussing his book. "She certainly writes well," said one of the young ladies. The eavesdropping author determined then and there to select a more fitting name for himself.

Earlier in his life, residents of the part of Zanesville known as The Terrace had given him a nickname which undoubtedly resulted indirectly from his being named Pearl. Despite his obviously feminine name, Pearl Grey was one hundred percent boy. He was not a bad boy, but in his efforts to live down the name that had been

6

given him, he sometimes leaned over backwards. His acts of inexplicable aggression and violence gave rise to his first sobriquet, "The Terror of the Terrace."

To live up to his title, Pearl organized gangs of young daredevils who terrorized the community with their vandalism. In their milder moods they foraged through the woods hunting birds and squirrels and vying with each other for honors in marksmanship, or spent peaceful hours fishing in the Licking and Muskingum Rivers that converge at Zanesville. But these were not the acts that characterized the gang or won the ringleader his reputation. There were sprees of smashing windows, breaking into vacant houses, raiding melon patches, robbing hen-roosts, and acts of wanton destructiveness. Whether the misdemeanors were committed by individuals or by the entire group, the blame generally fell on the shoulders of Pearl Grey.

Older residents of Zanesville still recall the pranks of "Young Doc" Grey. Old Mr. Bailey, the founder of the Zanesville Historical and Art Institute, had a special grudge against Pearl Grey. He could never forget that Pearl was the boy who had deliberately—and for no fathomable reason—destroyed a whole bed of tulips which Mr. Bailey had imported from Holland and planted on the Institute's flawless lawn. Teachers always recalled confiscating the dime novels to which Pearl was addicted, and which he distributed all too generously among his classmates at Zanesville High School. His classmates recall that their parents often forbade them to travel in the company of Pearl Grey, for to do so invariably led to a series of minor catastrophes, if not to major disaster.

Despite parental restrictions, however, there was always a goodly following in The Terrace Gang, for Pearl

7

was not only a born leader but he possessed the kind of daredevil spirit that never failed to find adventure. Among his disciples were Charlie Shaw, Ed McCaddon, Sam Playford, Harry Snell, Keith Van Horn, Tay Mohler, and Al Andrews, all old faithfuls during the reign of terror. Some of them are still living in Zanesville and enjoy reminiscing of the good old days—of fishing trips to Joe's Run and Dillon Falls, of excursions through the woods, of baseball games in McIntire Park. They remember that The Terror of the Terrace loved to roam through the woods dressed as an Indian, or spend hours lying on the riverbank daydreaming.

One of his closest friends, Charlie Shaw, kept in touch with him through correspondence for fifty years, after both had left Zanesville. Shaw sometimes shared his correspondence and reminiscences with the hometown newspapers. In 1934 he wrote:

"A few days ago I had a letter from Zane Grey ('Pearl' Grey, as the Zanesville gang knew him 48 years ago). He had been to the South Seas on a fishing trip and with the letter was a photo of himself and a monster sailfish he had landed on a light line. Someone had asked me how old Zane was and I told them he and I were within one month of the same age. I asked Grey about this in another letter and he replied that he had had no birthdays since he was 38. Zane used me as a character in two short stories he wrote, once in 'The Terrace Gang,' and again in 'Fisherman.' . . .

"Pearl (or Zane) was always interested in mounds. He said they were built by the Indians, no matter what kind of a mound it was. In their back yard where they lived at that time on Convers avenue,

I had often noticed a mound and Zane had reminded me on different occasions that it had been built by the Indians. It was covered with grass, and as I was not interested in mounds, I did not attempt to argue the matter.

"One day Pearl came to my home . . . in great excitement. He said that his father had consented to let him explore the Indian mound in their back yard and that if I would help him, I could share in the tomahawks, bows and arrows, flints, etc. that we would dig up.

"I consented eagerly and for three days we worked like troopers, spreading a pile of old ashes over the yard. It seems that his father had offered him a new suit of clothes if he would tear down the old ashpile and spread it out. But I have said that I knew nothing about mounds and Grey did. . . ."

Charlie bore no grudge against his friend for the ruse of the mound. In fact, it stood him in good stead. For Charlie had borrowed a stack of Pearl's Jesse James and Deadwood Dick novels and, while the books were in his possession, Charlie's mother had confiscated them and burned them. Charlie understood how much these literary treasures meant to Pearl, and he was convinced that he would never have been forgiven for their loss if he had not proved to be such a valuable assistant in "exploring the mound" in the Greys' back yard.

The Pitcher

Whatever Pearl Grey set out to do, he became completely absorbed in it and aimed at perfection. When he became a baseball player and enthusiast, he worked doggedly at his pitching until he developed a curve ball that baffled every batter who faced him. It was baseball that brought him successfully out of the adolescent phase and led him straight to his college career.

Pearl and his younger brother, "Reddy," often played baseball with the fellows in McIntire Park long before their high school days. After Pearl had become a student at the high school on Park Street, he and his brother, along with some other participants in the McIntire Park games, including Ed McCaddon, moved on to bigger things and joined the Zanesville amateur team, engaging in games with out-of-town teams.

The exchange games with other teams provided not only a healthy athletic competition but a new kind of social life for The Terror of the Terrace. Gradually he abandoned his more destructive pastimes and became a less aggressive boy. Misunderstood he may have been, but among his baseball cronies he was liked and admired.

Through his prowess as a pitcher, he had made himself an invaluable asset to the local team and, thus established as a highly acceptable member of a recognized social group, he closed the door on his outlaw days. He entered into the baseball dinners and after-the-game parties in good spirit and enjoyed his new place in Zanesville life.

With the establishment of his reputation as an athlete, Pearl even lost self-consciousness over his effeminate name. Excelling in an all-American, masculine sport, he no longer took a defensive attitude about his name. In fact, he began to capitalize on it with a typically adolescent zest for dramatization: he affected pearl-grey wearing apparel. Ed McCaddon, who still lives in Zanesville, recalls a social evening following a game with an out-of-town team when Pearl had to excuse himself from the dinner table to go home and change clothes. He had spilled chowder on his immaculate pearl-grey suit.

Pearl was still in high school and giving promise of being professional baseball material when the Grey family left Zanesville to take up residence in Columbus, Ohio. Pearl's fame as a pitcher went with him and he was soon pitching for Columbus games, which attracted scouts from various colleges and some of the big league teams.

The highlight of his early career in baseball occurred in the small town of Baltimore, Ohio, where he made baseball history and laid the foundations for his college life. Later, in an autobiographical sketch for *The American Magazine*, Zane Grey described the event with a vividness and humor that caught the imagination of every reader, whether baseball fan or not. The tale deserves repetition:

"One summer day, my cousin Jean and I journeyed to a little country town in Ohio named Baltimore, to drum up trade for my father, who assuredly needed it badly enough. This visit of ours occurred on a Saturday; and while Jean was out attending to business, I made the discovery that a baseball game was to be played that afternoon, between Baltimore and a rival village named Jacktown.

"Now it happened that Jacktown had never been beaten in a baseball game. Naturally, this aroused my curiosity and defiance. The idea! An unbeatable country-jake baseball team! I lost at once any interest in drumming up trade, and became obsessed with the idea of getting into that baseball game, to pitch for Baltimore.

"I talked with natives, visitors, players; and the more I talked the more keenly I wanted to play. Finally, I ran into a man I knew, Professor Hoskinson. He was principal of the village school at Baltimore, and had been a teacher in the Zanesville High School. Did he recognize me? He certainly did. Any teacher in Zanesville who ever had the misfortune to have me as a pupil was not likely to forget it.

"Now, as luck would have it, Professor Hoskinson was the catcher for the Baltimore baseball team, and my idea of pitching for that team appealed to him tremendously. But the drawback was—could he catch the curve balls I threw? He doubted it. We hunted up the Baltimore captain, unfolded our dire plot to defeat the great Jacktown nine. Whereupon the Baltimore captain became, for the time being, a wildly raving man, insane over the possibility of beating Jacktown. The thing to do was to get to a lonesome place and ascertain if Professor Hoskinson could catch my curve balls.

"It was a painful ordeal for the professor; but he was game, and what balls he could not catch he blocked with some part of his anatomy. I decided that he could do

Zane Grey

Even at the age of sixty Zane Grey could outlast many a younger man in the saddle.

Zane Grey was proud of the fact that a trace of
Indian blood flowed in his veins.

well enough. We planned then to keep my identity a secret. In baseball parlance I was what is called a 'ringer.'

"By now the town was baseball mad. Nevertheless I kept my secret from Jean; and after lunch, when he went back to the drumming job, I followed the crowd to the baseball ground.

"It was a large meadow on the outskirts of town, adjoining an endless corn field. When I looked at that corn field, eyeing the distance from the home plate and calculating if I could hit a ball into it, little did I dream what that corn field was to save me.

"The diamond was scalped, and there was a rude backstop and bleachers. No baseball crowd so wild and enthusiastic as a country one! All of Baltimore, Jacktown, and their environs appeared to be there. And no one thought Baltimore had a chance to win the game.

"In a huge barn at the side of the meadow I donned the Baltimore baseball suit of white canton flannel, with red stripes and letters. Fortunately, Hoskinson had a pair of spiked shoes, which he lent me. The other Baltimore players, assembled in the barn, were full of suppressed excitement. They all knew about the 'ringer,' and had read in the Columbus papers about my pitching. While we held a whispered consultation, a roar from the field heralded the arrival of the Jacktown nine.

"They appeared to be a husky lot of farmer boys, except the pitcher, who was a grown man, and a giant. He weighed three hundred pounds. He was the Jacktown blacksmith.

"Jacktown brought its own umpire. This individual fascinated me. He wore a jaunty cap with a tassel, a white blouse with tie, short pants of velveteen, white stockings, with low shoes and big buckles. I was so overcome at sight of him that I hardly thought about what kind of an umpire he would make. But I was destined to learn that he was the autocrat of this game, the paramount attraction, the beginning and the end.

"Baltimore had the first inning at bat, with Jacktown in the field. The giant pitcher delivered a ball, and never before had I seen its like for speed.

" 'O-n-e s-t-r-i-kk-ee!' bawled the umpire.

"Our side went out—one, two, three—and only one of our men hit the ball at all.

"But when I faced these husky players, wielding their bats as if they were pitch-forks, I knew I had them utterly at my mercy. Using a wide outcurve and a drop curve, alternating them, I struck out the first three Jacktown players in nine pitched balls. How that Baltimore crowd yelled, whistled, screamed, and shrieked!

"After another inning for us at bat, in which I faced the Jacktown pitcher and gauged his terrific speed, I decided Baltimore could never effectively hit his pitching. In our turn at field I disposed of the next three Jacktown men as I had the first. This fact began to stagger them. Then, on our third turn at bat, I called our players aside and whispered emphatic instructions.

" 'Don't swing at his balls. Choke your bat short and poke at them. Just lay your bat as if you wanted to stop them. Then run—run!'

"My ruse worked beautifully. The giant pitcher did not know what a bunt was. He was so heavy he could not run up on a little dumpy ball rolling on the ground. As a result, two of the Baltimore players got on base. The next one fouled out; and the following struck out, trying to bunt. But the next man laid down a teasing roller to the third baseman. He dove for it and threw it wild. Then other Jacktown players threw wild.

"The result was the Baltimore men scored, and a third

was safe at second. Our next batter got in front of one of those terrific pitches and was hit. I expected it to kill him, but he took his base in great glee. The next batter bunted another that the huge pitcher could not handle in time.

"Thus it was I found myself at bat with three men on bases. I made up my mind just to meet one of the Jacktown pitcher's straight swift balls. I missed the first two. Indeed, they looked like peas as they zipped by me. But I hit the next one. It went like a shot, over the center fielder, and over the fence into the corn field.

"The Baltimore crowd went crazy.

"Our next man struck out. The game went on. Jacktown swung widely and helplessly at my curve balls. They were mystified. The giant pitcher, who was evidently a great hitter, roared with rage after swinging at my balls and missing them so strangely. All the Jacktown players crowded behind the plate to watch me pitch, sure now that something was wrong.

"We scored no more. In the seventh inning, when again I struck out three more men, the jaunty umpire ran out before the crowd and bawled, '*Game called! Nine to nothing! Favor Jacktown!* . . . *Baltimore pitcher uses a crooked ball!*'

"At that, pandemonium broke loose. Fearing a riot, I ran toward the barn to get into my clothes. Never before had I heard such an uproar. When I got half undressed, who should appear but Cousin Jean, breathless and wild with excitement.

" 'You've got to run!' he panted. 'Jacktown players— going to ride you on a rail—and tar and feather you! Never mind your clothes. Run!'

"In great perturbation I peered out of the barn door. What should I see but the giant pitcher, carrying a rail over his shoulder, striding toward the barn, followed by the other Jacktown players and a yelling mob.

"I snatched my trousers and leaped out to run across the field. The giant and his followers roared and gave pursuit. Run! I flew. And as I was unhampered by any clothes, except shirt and shoes, I could better imitate the swiftness of a bird . . ."

The pitcher outran his pursuers and hid out in the corn field all day. Toward evening he ventured forth and finally met his cousin Jean at a station along the railroad. The tragi-comic story might have been soon forgotten except for its sequel. A University of Pennsylvania scout had observed the game at Baltimore, learned the identity of the pitcher, and traced him to Columbus some weeks later. It was he who persuaded the boy to choose Pennsylvania for his college training.

That same fall, Pearl Grey registered as a freshman at the University of Pennsylvania.

College Days

Life is a series of challenges and adjustments to changing situations. In the Nineties, even as today, the transition from high school to college life presented a difficult adjustment. Pearl Grey never dodged a challenge, but neither did he adjust himself satisfactorily to college life. When he graduated in 1896 it was with combined feelings of relief and reluctance.

He had never been a scholar. He read widely, but he liked to read independently. His mind flitted from daydreams to essential realities and back to daydreams again, never contented to be pinned down to the discipline of concentration. Sitting in the stuffy lecture halls he let his mind wander to the woods and rivers while the voice of the lecturer droned on, disturbing him only very slightly.

He was happy in the college library. It was a quiet refuge where he could escape for a time to dream of the kind of life he would have preferred, or to read from his favorite authors. He was not really a lazy student, though he may have given that impression. A more accurate description of his attitude might include the words "willful" and "moody." He studied hard, on occasion; but he studied only what he wanted to study and when he felt like studying. His voluntary study of literature far exceeded any assigned materials in his English courses, for he read the works of Victor Hugo, the essays of Robert Louis Stevenson, the prose and poetry of Poe and Kipling. He devoured Fenimore Cooper and Scott; these he considered his favorites, but he felt he learned more from Stevenson. Poetry held a strong appeal for him and he took pleasure in memorizing long passages from Tennyson, Wordsworth, Coleridge, and Matthew Arnold, whose "*Dover Beach*" was one of Grey's favorite poems throughout life. Though his literary leanings were to the romantic side, he showed great variety in reading tastes, for he delved deeply into scientific treatises, notably the works of Darwin. He read every available book on the technical aspects of writing, for already he had begun to nurture the ambition to write. But he was repelled by contemporary fiction and felt that he could never write in the "modern" manner, for the trend was toward a realism that always sent him back to the old masters of the romantic school.

Among his schoolmates, except on the ball diamond, he was ill at ease and apparently as misunderstood as he had been in the days of the cave. He started off on the wrong foot, making the grave error of infringing upon upperclass territory in the lecture room on the first day of classes. He did it innocently, unaware of the rules of "hazing" and the sharp dividing line between freshmen and upperclassmen. But his innocent act caused a riot during which the lecture-room was wrecked and the offending freshman lost every stitch of his clothing, including his shoes and his watch. He escaped to his room, feeling fortunate that he had not been torn literally limb from limb.

But that was only the beginning of a series of innocent blunders. Having antagonized the sophomores the first day, he was over-cautious in observing the class distinctions, and in paying particular attention to one detail of behavior, he was likely to neglect another. The worst mistake was in passing through a corridor that was reserved for upperclassmen. He was utterly bewildered when a horde of upperclassmen chased him out of the building and through the streets.

On this occasion, however, fortune smiled on him. Fortune in this case took the form of two grocery boys, carrying between them a basket of potatoes. Grey promptly appropriated the basket of potatoes, took up his stand at the head of a flight of narrow stairs, and dared his pursuers to attack. With mad shouts, they started up the steps, but their yells of rage and defiance soon turned to yells of pain. They were taken completely unaware by this madcap freshman, who could hurl potatoes as well as a baseball—they had not dreamed that the object of their attack was a crack pitcher.

The freshman left a heap of sophomores piled up on the stairs and ran to his room to brood over his fate. He took no pride in his brilliant self-defense, for he realized that when the news of the melée reached the ears of the school authorities, he would be expelled and sent home in disgrace. He had bitter regrets for himself and for his family. For his own part, he had borrowed money and had vowed not only to make a success of his college career but to make the varsity nine as well. But worst of all was the disappointment in store for his family, for Doc Grey confidently expected that his eldest son would follow in his footsteps in dental practice.

It was one of the darkest moments of the young man's life. He was filled with stubbornness and determination, but he knew defeat when he saw it.

There was a knock at the door, and he knew that the hour of his formal dismissal from the University of Pennsylvania was at hand. With a heavy heart he answered the sharp summons.

His guest did not have the appearance of a college official. He wore a slouchy hat at a rakish angle on one side of his head and held a smouldering cigar at much the same angle between his teeth. Without a word he removed his overcoat and hat and laid a hand on the student's right arm.

"Where'd you get the whip?" he demanded abruptly.

The astonished Grey was incapable of understanding or even of making a coherent reply.

"The wing, boy! The arm!" said his visitor. "Where'd you learn to peg like that?"

Grey realized then that his visitor must have witnessed his potato battle with the sophomores, but his numb brain could not explain the visitor's identity or his interest. Stammering, he told the man how he had developed the "wing" as a boy, throwing pebbles, walnuts, ripe tomatoes, or whatever missiles were at hand. The man's keen eyes were appraising the lad as he spoke, and yet he did not seem unfriendly.

"So that explains it!" he exclaimed, shifting the cigar to the other corner of his mouth. "Well, that was quite a show you put on today. The sophs will never forget it —or forgive it either, for that matter."

Then just as the boy was beginning to wonder whether the college employed detectives to handle such cases as this, his caller went on: "I've heard all about your pitching out in Ohio. . . . You report to the training cage in February."

Not until then did the frightened boy have the nerve to ask the mysterious visitor to identify himself.

"I'm Irwin," said the man impatiently. "Your potato fight this afternoon convinced me we need you on the varsity. But keep it under your hat."

He vanished as abruptly as he had entered, leaving the student to ponder over the events of the day and the possibilities of the future. His visitor was none other than Arthur Irwin, famed in professional baseball and coach at Pennsylvania. And he had come in person to offer a strange freshman a place on the varsity! This could be the turning point that would make his entire college experience worth while!

In the midst of these dreams of pitching for varsity victory, the boy stopped short to face realities. It was much more likely that he would be expelled from the university tomorrow, and not even be on hand for spring training. If the coach had heard of the potato fight, the dean assuredly had, too.

But the days went by and, except for constant heckling from vengeful sophomores, the incident seemed to have been forgotten. Pearl's luck had changed at last, and in the spring he found himself quite at home with his teammates.

He still was a misfit as far as the student body in general was concerned. He lacked the capacity for making friends except under the give-and-take conditions of athletic competition. He was befriended by the varsity catcher, Danny Coogan, who sponsored him for membership in Sigma Nu. Not only fellow baseball players but athletes from the football and track teams became his friends. He was flattered when the famous football center, Al Bull, who had helped to defeat Yale, Princeton and Harvard, chose him for a roommate.

Scholastically he never improved. The confinement of the classroom was too much for him and he despaired of ever making a good showing, even in the literature courses that he liked. Although he continued to work toward the degree in dentistry to please his father, he still clung secretly to his desire to be a writer. He wrote countless stories and articles about his summer fishing jaunts and submitted them to various outdoor magazines without success. So he plodded along with his examinations and somehow managed to scrape through.

When he was graduated in 1896 it was not with a feeling of pride in his accomplishment, but with the sneaking suspicion that the professors had read his examination papers with one eye shut and the other half-blinded by pity.

The Lean Years

Regardless of his scholastic failings, Pearl Grey was doubtless a competent dentist. In later years he sometimes remarked jestingly that the days of his dental practice were "pretty rough—on the patients." But the jest belies his true nature, for he was precise, accurate, and conscientious in everything he undertook and his pride in workmanship was such that he was never satisfied with half-measures. Moreover, success in the dental profession was something he felt he owed to his father and to his brother, R.C., who gave him the financial backing required to set him up in practice in New York.

R.C. was making a far more comfortable living at professional baseball than was his elder brother at dentistry, a fact which probably rankled, particularly in view of the fact that Pearl had never wanted to be a dentist and had always been happy on a ball diamond. After his graduation he had become a member of the Orange Athletic Club of East Orange, New Jersey, and when he found the income from dental practice was too meager for decent subsistence he determined to play professional baseball in the summer so that he could afford to practice dentistry in the winter. His first experience with professional ball was with the Eastern League, but he felt the tendency to gravitate back toward his home state. He went first to the Tri-State League and later traveled as far west as Jackson, Michigan, in a transfer to the Michigan League.

He found that he was looking forward more and more to summer vacations and the baseball season as a release from his professional duties. He disliked New York intensely; he hated his miserable hall bedroom; he chafed at the inactive life he was leading. He was sorely tempted to accept some of the attractive offers to join the major leagues, but his parents persuaded him to abandon professional baseball. Eventually his longing for adventure and his fever to write became overpowering. In 1904 he closed his dental office, for better or for worse, and concentrated on becoming a writer.

He had continued his vacation trips, fishing, canoeing, hunting, even during the months when he played baseball, and he had had reasonable success in selling the few articles he had written about these summer adventures, notably his articles on black bass which were published by *Field and Stream*. After the acceptance of his first article, "A Day on the Delaware," in 1902, he had been encouraged to persevere along that line. But he wanted to produce something more ambitious than that. He thought he should write books. His brother Reddy encouraged him, but it was his mother who provided the suggestion he needed to start him on the right track.

Mrs. Grey had one day discovered, in a pile of rubbish she was burning in the back yard, a mouldy old notebook that had belonged to her grandfather, the pioneer Ebenezer Zane. It was a carefully-written diary, including the founding of Fort Henry on the Ohio frontier on the site where the city of Wheeling, West Virginia, is now located, and the heroism of Colonel Zane's sister, Betty, who risked her life to bring ammunition into the fort when it was besieged by Indians and British in 1782.

Mrs. Grey rightly surmised that the diary would be of interest and value to her son, Pearl, for he had fed upon stories of his Zane forefathers from the time of his early childhood when his grandmother had held him spellbound with tales of pioneer days, and particularly of her own childhood memories of Betty Zane. Later, during his school days, Pearl learned that these ancestors of his played important parts in the making of early American history; that it was this same great-grandfather, Ebenezer Zane, who had blazed the trail through the wilderness from West Virginia to the present site of Maysville, Kentucky, which became known as "Zane's Trace," the road by which immigrant farmers traveled to open up the fertile farmlands of the Ohio Valley. It was the same Colonel Zane for whom Zanesville was named, and in whose honor a monument in the Walnut Grove Cemetery of Martins Ferry, Ohio, was inscribed:

In memory of
Ebenezer Zane,
who died 19th November, 1812,
in the 66th year of his age.
He was the first permanent inhabitant of this part of
the western world, having first begun to reside here
in 1769. He died as he lived, an honest man.

The diary of this famed ancestor was a wealth of family and national history. Pearl pored over the musty pages learning of the hardships of the early Zanes, of their way of life, their personalities and foibles. Most intriguing to him was the character of Betty Zane, her fiery courage, her independent spirit, her well-known feat of heroism in running through the thick of Indian rifle-fire with an apronful of powder to replenish Fort Henry's exhausted ammunition supply. She was more than a legendary figure. Out of the pages of her brother's diary she emerged, a real flesh-and-blood woman, with all her captivating charm and all her willfulness. Her romance was woven vividly upon the background of the pioneer scene.

So it happened that Pearl Grey spent an entire New York winter reading of the exploits of his famous ancestors and re-writing the story of Betty Zane in the form of a historical novel that was to bear her name. It was hard work. Writing did not come easily to him, nor were his surroundings overly inspiring. Much of his work was done on an uncomfortably empty stomach; it was not unusual for him to go without food for a day or two at a time. He was secluded in a hall bedroom within a stone's throw of the roaring elevated railway. The room was drab and cold, and its only redeeming feature was the constant presence of a huge tomcat who served a dual function of companion and mouser. The latter was probably more important, for the mice that held night sessions on the bedroom floor had a peculiar appetite for manuscript paper.

A man with less perseverance or with a less active imagination would surely have given up in the face of such adversities, but Grey labored doggedly on. Battles between tomcat and mice continued unnoticed and the "L" trains rushed by unheard. The writer was lost to his immediate surroundings. He was standing on a rocky bluff with Ebenezer Zane, glimpsing for the first time the beauties of the Ohio River and visualizing the wealth of resources in the valley beyond. He was stalking through the woods with his idol, Lew Wetzel, canny hunter and Indian scout. He was feasting on wild turkey and hot biscuits at the Zane table, with Ebenezer and his pioneer wife, his brothers, Silas, Jonathan, and Isaac, Isaac's beautiful Indian-princess wife, and Elizabeth Zane, the youngest of the family, pampered and spoiled by her older brothers, but a lovable young lady nonetheless.

During that frigid New York winter, Pearl Grey warmed his room with the campfires of Indian fighters and hunters on the trail, and with the flames from a log fire crackling on the open hearth of a pioneer cabin. He peopled his bleak world with redskins and redcoats, with British traitors, border renegades, and pioneer heroes and heroines. He re-lived the building of Fort Henry, the farthest outpost of the Virginia border, and fought for its survival through siege after siege until the final victory was won in the last battle of the American Revolution. He wrote the story as he lived it, and when the manuscript was finished he knew that it was good.

To convince publishers of the merits of his work was another matter. The young writer made the rounds in a vain quest for a publisher who shared his belief in himself. Literally dozens of them refused the manuscript, a situation that was far more discouraging than the privations of the winter months during which the romance of Betty Zane was written. Undaunted, Grey talked with a wealthy patient who had sufficient confidence in his dentist's writing ability to lend him money for publication of the book. So the author had his work published, at his own expense, by the Charles Francis Press in New York City.

Despite the skepticism of publishers, the mere fact that he had completed a book and had seen it in print gave new courage to the writer. His dental practice, which had been secondary in importance for some time, was at last completely abandoned. It was a difficult decision to make, particularly in view of the disappointment it caused the elder Dr. Grey. He, like the publishers, doubted his son's ability to earn his way as an author; on the other hand, he had no doubt that dentistry would at least provide a decent living. He was not won over until Pearl sent him a copy of the newly published volume. Dr. Grey read it and re-read it; it came to occupy a place on his bookshelf next to the well-read Bible.

Mrs. Grey, too, was proud of her son's modest success —for the book was praised by reviewers—and undoubtedly the more so because the story was of her own ancestors, passed down through her own hands. She had taken such an active part in its creation that she felt justified in criticizing minor points of historical authenticity and interpretation. So well did she know her pioneer history that she immediately spotted an inaccuracy on page 111 of *Betty Zane* and wrote to her son, calling him to task for fixing the blame upon Michael Cresap for the murder of the family of Logan, the Mingo chief. She was correct. There had been considerable discussion of the incident and a number of historians had uncovered evidence establishing the innocence of Cresap.

On the whole, however, the book was accurate in detail. It was not a commercial success, for the printer lacked the channels for placing it before the public to best advantage. Those who read it invariably praised it, and it was always with a sense of mingled embarrassment and pride that the author occasionally overheard discussions of his work.

Not long after the publication of his first book, Pearl Grey locked the door on his dental office for the last time. At the same time he turned his back on his profession, he turned his back on the given name, Pearl. As "Zane Grey," he left the city and went with his mother, his brothers and sister, to live in the country and write. He had little but his faith in himself—and his family's faith in him—to see him through, for *Betty Zane* was still selling very slowly in 1904.

As proof that the writer's self-evaluation was valid, *Betty Zane* has been reprinted many times and is still selling. The plates were finally purchased from the original printer and resold to a publishing house at a neat profit. In 1928 the author wrote: "I sometimes wonder how it would have affected me if the comfortable little income the book now brings had been received in the leaner years."

Buffalo Jones

During the lonely years at college and the lean years in New York, Zane Grey had cherished a dream of romance. His daydreams were not always of the woods and the fields. Against this setting there frequently appeared the vision of the blue-eyed, flaxen-haired heroine of "Jim of the Cave," the home-town girl with whom he had gone to school and whom he had worshiped from afar, too shy to make himself known to her.

But when romance comes to a man in real life, it is seldom as he had dreamed it. The girl who won his heart was not the blonde princess, remote and forbidding, but a brown-haired girl with a friendly manner and an open, unforgettable smile. She was a student at Hunter College in New York City when she met young Dr. Grey and learned of his determination, his hopes and dreams, and his discouragements. She had more faith in his future than he himself had. She was a constant source of inspiration.

They became engaged before she graduated from Hunter. There was a long year during which they saw little of each other, while Zane lived in the country cottage with his family and tried to prove himself as a writer. Then in the autumn of 1905, the home-town papers in Zanesville bore headlines:

HAPPILY WEDDED
Dr. P. Zane Grey, Author of
Betty Zane, Weds Miss Roth in New York City.

The news story continued:

"This announcement received in this city is of interest to many people in Eastern Ohio:

Mrs. Lina Roth
announces the marriage of her daughter,
Lina Elise,
to
Dr. Zane Grey
on Tuesday, November the twenty-first,
nineteen hundred and five,
New York City.

"Dr. Grey is the author of 'Betty Zane,' one of the most popular stories ever read in this section of Ohio. It will be gratifying to his many friends to know that the doctor is now engaged on a companion book to 'Betty Zane' and the manuscript will be delivered to the publisher probably before the close of the holidays."

The manuscript referred to in the news item was *The Spirit of the Border*, another historical novel based on Zane family history and relating more of the heroic deeds of Lew Wetzel, the Indian scout. Although the manuscript was finished in 1905, it was not published until the following year.

Zane Grey went with his bride, whom he always

called "Dolly," to live at Lackawaxen, Pennsylvania, in a small cottage overlooking the Delaware River where he and his brothers had spent many happy summer days fishing and roaming through the woods. "Here," the author wrote later, "I had the first happy times since early childhood; and I had them, despite lack of money or the encouragement of recognition. The spring days, with the smell of burning forests in the air; the pale blossoms of trailing arbutus peeping from the dead leaves; the white pines and the brown aisles; the lonely silence of the hills, where the purple aster and fringed gentian waved in the wind; the alder swales deep in the woods, where the deer browsed and the grouse drummed —from close association with these I grew toward a fulfillment of love of nature."

The winter months, when ice and sleet made walks through the woods impossible, provided an excellent opportunity for reading the works that Zane had always wanted to read. He and his wife studied together and discussed the things they read. As his knowledge of writing and writers increased, his determination to join the ranks of the literary profession grew. He experimented with all kinds of self-expression: articles, short stories, romances, and even verse. As months went by with no further recognition of his ability, his wife's confidence never diminished. She not only encouraged him; she insisted that he persevere, even when their funds were exhausted.

A successful writer must have a dual personality, combining the practical and the impractical; the hard-headed business manager and the sensitive creator; the disciplined worker and the undisciplined dreamer. Dolly Grey was a perfect complement to such a personality. When Zane's practical nature urged him to give up the apparently unfounded belief in his future career in writing, she refused to listen, and reaffirmed her own belief. She appointed herself "business manager" to leave his mind and time free to try out all the forms of writing that interested him. She went over all his manuscripts with him and offered constructive criticism; later she assumed all responsibility for revisions, so that her husband never had to revise a manuscript after the first draft. She dipped into her own savings and ran the household with careful economy to stretch the funds over the maximum period of time. She insisted that *The Spirit of the Border* be published, even at the expense of their own meagre funds. She arranged to keep the house quiet and as comfortable as possible during scheduled writing hours so that idle-hour daydreams could be turned into hand-written pages.

When Dolly's savings as well as her husband's were practically gone, and a boy, named Romer Zane, was born, Zane decided to give up his fruitless efforts toward becoming a writer and turn to something that would provide a steady income for his family. Dolly steadfastly refused. "Even when our fortunes were at lowest ebb," wrote Zane, "she always cheered me, made me believe what in my soul I knew."

The Grey fortunes were, indeed, at low ebb when a coincidence changed Zane's whole way of life as well as that of his family. Notwithstanding perseverance and immense courage, it is still quite possible that Zane Grey would eventually have returned to dental practice—or even to professional baseball—had he not chanced to meet Buffalo Jones.

Among Zane's acquaintances was Alvah James, a man who had gained some credit for his exploring excursions in South American countries. James knew Col. C. J.

Jones, the great plainsman who had predicted the extinction of the American buffalo and had done all in his power to prevent the occurrence of such a catastrophe. Formerly a buffalo hunter in the great West, Jones had lost his taste for the kill and had devoted his life to the study and preservation of the wild animals he admired, chief among them the buffalo. It was thus that he had gained his nickname.

Buffalo Jones embarked on a project of hybridization of buffalo with black Galloway cattle in the belief that he could produce a breed capable of withstanding the rigors of desert life, feeding solely on the natural vegetation and making the relatively long treks to water supplies. He proved his theory, although at great cost and with many setbacks. He established a ranch on the rim of the Grand Canyon and stocked it with prize Galloway cattle. Then, with the aid of expert cowhands, he rounded up herds of wild buffalo grazing on the plains of Montana.

The first great problem he had faced was that of transportation. He had anticipated the great expense of shipping herds of buffalo by rail across the mountains to his ranch. But he had not anticipated that the hardy buffalo, who calmly stood stockstill through a desert dust-storm or a severe blizzard, would die as a result of a mere ride in a box-car. Load after load of buffalo were shipped, with the same heart-breaking result each time. After many attempts, one of Jones's assistants found the solution: the buffalo could travel only by night. They were permitted to rest in the daytime and successfully accomplished the trip to the ideal range by slow, easy stages at night.

Jones called his new breed "cattalo." They were rugged animals, with remarkable powers of endurance and digestion. They required no "artificial" feed and did not need to be sheltered. In contrast to domestic cattle, the cattalo had fourteen pairs of ribs, which added to their strength. Their hide was as luxurious and as valuable commercially as that of any wild buffalo, and most important of all, their meat was even more tasty.

The success of the experiment was most satisfying to Buffalo Jones and his fellow workers; so much so, in fact, that they were eager to expand their stock and continue with further experimentation. This required more capital than Jones possessed, after the tremendous losses he had incurred as a result of the transportation problem. So he made a trip East to raise money, using as a drawing card motion pictures he had taken of wild animals he had captured with the use of a lasso.

Alvah James and his enthusiastic young friend, Zane Grey, were members of a New York audience viewing the amazing pictures and listening to the incredible stories told by Buffalo Jones. Unfortunately, the stories were far too incredible to be digested by an audience of city slickers who were suspicious of Westerners and their tall tales. While Grey listened with bated breath, others around him, including Eastern sportsmen of some note, were listening with their tongues in their cheeks. Buffalo Jones was stamped as an eccentric and a gross liar.

When Zane Grey went home to his Lackawaxen cottage, he found that the old plainsman had so captured his imagination and won his sympathy that he could think of nothing else. He longed to lead the adventurous life that Buffalo Jones had lived and described so graphically. More than that, he wanted to help the older man lick his financial problem and, at the same time, prove to the world that his stories were true.

Back to New York he went and, overcoming his natural diffidence as best he could, went to call on Buffalo Jones in his room at the Grand Hotel. Jones was a sick man, alone in a big city. Zane Grey stayed with him for a time, took care of him and made him comfortable. What was more important, perhaps, he convinced the old man that a few people—himself included—gave full credence to the stories of roping wild animals, and that proof could be furnished for the benefit of skeptics.

"Take me back with you," Zane urged. "Let me go West with you and see it at first hand. I'll write about it and prove to the public that you *can* capture wild animals with a lasso."

Jones was pleased and flattered, but he, like the publishers, was not persuaded of Grey's ability as an author. "Bring me something you have written," he said.

Zane produced a copy of *Betty Zane* and left Jones to read it and consider the proposition.

When Zane himself reconsidered the possibility of such an expedition, he was assailed by great doubts. He had made claims that he surely would be unable to fulfill. Jones would soon see that the man who wrote *Betty Zane* could not possibly write of the Far West, of which he had no knowledge or understanding. How could he have presumed even to make such a suggestion?

Feeling foolish and defeated, he returned to Lackawaxen without saying good-bye to Colonel Jones. He could not even bring himself to discuss it with his wife at first, but at length he told her of his meeting with the plainsman and confessed the wild scheme that he had entertained briefly, only to give it up when he faced the fact that it was beyond his power ever to realize such a far-fetched goal.

Dolly Grey listened silently to the whole outpouring of the birth and death of this great plan. Then to his great surprise she upbraided him—not for being carried away by his youthful zeal, not for dreaming of leaving his family for Western adventures, but for admitting defeat without even giving his plan a fair hearing.

"Go back to New York at once," she concluded.

Her husband regarded her with amazement. In five years of repeated trials and failures, he had produced only two insignificant books and a handful of articles for *Field and Stream*, thereby proving that he could never support a family with his writing. But in five years' time, her faith in him was greater than ever. The least he could do for her was to keep faith in himself.

Prepared to argue, to plead his case as eloquently as the occasion required, he returned to New York and inquired at the Grand Hotel for Buffalo Jones. As he spoke, a heavy hand fell on his shoulder with a resounding slap that nearly sent him spinning across the room.

"Boy!" said the familiar voice of Buffalo Jones. "Where did you learn to write like that?"

The Turn of the Tide

From the degrees of enthusiasm that accompanied the plans for the Westward trek, it would have been difficult to ascertain which was younger, Zane Grey or Buffalo Jones. The old man, then in his seventies, was rejuvenated with the prospect of returning to his old stamping ground and, incidentally, of redeeming his reputation for veracity. To the younger man, the whole thing was surrounded with a dream-like aura.

Buffalo Jones went on ahead, after arranging to meet Zane in Arizona the following spring. Left without the older man's guidance and enthusiasm to buoy him up, Zane once more fell into a morass of despair. In the midst of his wild dreaming, he had forgotten that the project would cost money—for Jones himself was too hard-pressed to offer financial backing for the trip. An inventory of the Grey exchequer revealed the awful truth: the Western expedition would cost nearly every last penny the family possessed. It was, therefore, unthinkable. He would stay in the East, find work, assume his appropriate responsibilities as head of the family.

None of the pioneer wives of the ancestral Zanes could

have met this situation with greater calmness and fortitude than that displayed by Dolly Grey. "You *must* go," she said. "It would be unfair to Colonel Jones if you were to back out now. Don't worry about me; I'll get along somehow. Besides," she added thoughtfully, "something tells me that this trip West will be the turn of the tide for you."

Only the passage of years could prove how right she was. Zane Grey went West as a greenhorn Easterner. He viewed the West through Eastern eyes; he wrote about it for Eastern readers. That was the all-important factor in hitting his stride as a writer. Up to that time, there had really been nothing wrong with his writing except that he lacked the glamorous settings that would appeal to popular imagination. In the Eastern mind, the West was Utopia; it was a land of plenty and of free-handed hospitality; of rugged beauty and outdoor solitude, a land of growth and promise. Westerners themselves, as in the instance of Buffalo Jones, were frequently looked upon as tellers of tall tales, but to read of the exciting West as seen first-hand by a city-bred Easterner was both satisfying and reassuring. There were, after all, fresh fields to which one could escape—whether vicariously or actually—when the boredom of the conventional East became oppressive.

"No boy suddenly dropped into the West," wrote Grey, "could have had a more magnificent adventure than I had." Meeting Jones at Flagstaff, Arizona, in the spring, he joined Jones's caravan of Mormon plainsmen to cross the Painted Desert and the upper part of the Grand Canyon. After ten days on horseback, a grueling journey for an unseasoned rider like Grey, they arrived at House Rock Valley where Jones had established his "cattalo" ranch. Grey inspected the ranch with great interest and was amazed to learn that the twenty calves born that spring were expected to market at a total of ten thousand dollars.

The first night at the ranch was a thrilling experience for the tenderfoot. He was meeting at last with real pioneers and listening silently to talk of lions and cougars, wild-horse roundups and buffalo hunts. His companions were Texas rangers, hunters, cowhands, Indians, and Mormon guides who had learned to live on the desert. He would gladly have stayed on at the ranch for a time, but Jones had a pack of hounds all set to start on a lion-hunt the following morning.

Zane was reluctant to confess his physical state on being awakened at dawn. His bones ached, his muscles creaked, his lips were parched from the dryness of the desert, and he was struggling to throw off a cold. In that condition he could scarcely take great pleasure in anticipating another day spent on the back of a wild mustang, even for the sake of the long-awaited lion hunt.

To add to his discomfiture, one of the cowhands inquired pointedly, "Of course you can ride?"

Knowing Western standards of horsemanship and the scorn that would be occasioned if he were thrown from the back of a cayuse—"an unpardonable sin in Arizona"—he admitted the truth. The ranch hands were not unkind about it, but astonished to think that Buffalo Jones would permit anyone less than a good horseman to accompany him on a hunting expedition. With rugged Western humor, they selected Grey's mount from the corral—a high-strung spirited mustang of pure white. It was unquestionably the most beautiful animal on the entire ranch. What Grey did not know was that buffaloes have a peculiar aversion for white, and to ride past a buffalo herd on a white horse is tantamount to waving a red flag in front of a mad bull.

When Jones warned him of the stampede that might very well be caused by the sight of the white horse, Grey replied humorously that, since the horse was bound to throw him sooner or later anyway, it really didn't matter just how or when the incident occurred. As it turned out, the incident was averted by the practical joker who had chosen the white mustang for Grey; he arrived on the scene just in time to head off the angry buffalo as it charged upon the white horse and its paralyzed rider.

There were other close calls, but the tenderfoot soon learned that in the West hair-raising adventure is all in a day's work. He learned much more on the expedition. He learned how to handle horses and hounds. He learned the vagaries of Western climate and desert storms and how to combat the elements. He learned Buffalo Jones's admiration for wild animals and his singular repugnance at the thought of killing.

With Jones he crossed Buckskin Mountain and penetrated Buckskin Forest, where the goal of their journey was realized. With a pack of hounds leading the chase, they tracked down mountain lions and, true to his word, Buffalo Jones lassoed them and brought them back to camp alive. Armed with a camera, Zane Grey took pictures of the famous plainsman in action, capturing and subduing the magnificent wild beasts.

Although this was the highlight of the Western adventure, there were other incidents equally thrilling. They hunted, and nearly captured, the elusive White King, leader of a herd of wild mustang. They passed through desert storms and camped out on clear frosty nights after days spent hunting polar wolves. They skirted the rim of Grand Canyon and discovered the ruins of a forgotten Indian civilization: caves and temples and sepulchers. They tracked down the last herd of buffalo known to exist. The trail led them across country where hostile Comanches still roamed at large and when, after surviving many unforeseen hazards, they found the quarry, it marked the end of a two-year quest for Jones who had been told that he would never find "the last herd."

When Zane Grey and Buffalo Jones parted company, the latter was making eager plans to hunt and rope grizzly bears, a new experience for him. Grey was reluctant to miss this adventure, but the time had come for him to return to Lackawaxen and begin the record of his days with Buffalo Jones. It was not as pleasant to write the story as it was to live it, and it was several months before the manuscript of *The Last of the Plainsmen* was completed to the author's satisfaction. The task of writing may not have been easy, but neither was it dull, for as Grey remarked in the preface: "Happily in remembrance a writer can live over his experiences, and see once more the moon-blanched silver mountain peaks against the dark blue sky; hear the lonely sough of the night-wind through the pines; feel the dance of wild expectation in the quivering pulse; the stir, the thrill, the joy of hard action in perilous moments; the mystery of man's yearning for the unattainable."

As he wrote, he re-lived each day of the greatest experience of his life. And at the same time, he looked forward to his reunion with Buffalo Jones, who was returning to the East on affairs of business, among them the business of having *The Last of the Plainsmen* published.

It was Jones's idea to take the manuscript to Harper

and Brothers in New York, for he was acquainted with a member of the editorial staff, Mr. Ripley Hitchcock, and was certain that this would assure special consideration. Grey himself was not so optimistic. Ironically enough, this was the same Mr. Hitchcock who had already rejected four Zane Grey books, including *Betty Zane* and *The Spirit of the Border*. But this might be, as Dolly Grey had predicted, the turn of the tide. Together the two men called upon Mr. Hitchcock and presented the finished manuscript.

Hitchcock was so cordial and earnest in his reiterations that the book would be given the greatest attention that hope was reborn in the heart of the writer. It would be something like vindicating justice if the firm of Harper and Brothers, after four rejections, would be the first to accept one of his books. He returned to Lackawaxen to wait impatiently.

He had not long to wait. Within a few days a letter came from Harpers' asking him to come to the office on Franklin Square. It was a noncommittal letter, but mentioned that the purpose of the call was to discuss his manuscript. Could it be that his presence was required to arrange a publication contract? Once more he hurried to New York and was ushered into the office of Ripley Hitchcock.

The editor was friendly enough, but his reception was not as enthusiastic as it had been when Buffalo Jones had accompanied his young friend. He had asked Mr. Grey to come in to the office to receive his rejected manuscript in person. He was sorry that Harpers' could not use the story. He assured Mr. Grey that he had given the manuscript careful and attentive reading and in conclusion he added:

"I don't see anything in this to convince me you can write either narrative or fiction."

With the unconsciously cruel words of Ripley Hitchcock echoing in his ears, the writer stumbled wordlessly from the office in a state of extreme shock. His body was numb and cold, his vision blurred. Somehow he found his way to the street, his brain in a turmoil as he clutched the useless manuscript. Failure weighed so heavily upon him that he could no longer move under the great burden. Leaning blindly against an iron post on the corner of Pearl Street, he could see nothing but the black chaos of the dead dreams for which he and his wife had struggled and sacrificed.

His wife! How could he bring this news to her? Her hopes had been so high, her faith so unfaltering. *She* had said that this was to be the turn of the tide. Could she have been wrong?

No! She was not wrong. Hitchcock was wrong; the publishers were wrong. With the help and forebearance of his wife, he would prove that they were wrong.

When Dolly Grey predicted the turn of the tide, she had no way of foreseeing in what manner her prophecy would come true. But when her husband returned from New York with the rejected manuscript and a new light of determination in his eyes, she knew that he had won rather than lost. It was a psychological battle that really turned the tide, for until that time her husband's writing had been timid, half-apologetic, lacking in self-confidence. Now he was sure of himself and what he was going to do.

The Last of the Plainsmen went unacclaimed from publisher to publisher, but the adventure that had inspired it had left many an idea and inspiration in the mind of the writer. As rejection slips accumulated, he wrote and wrote. He was writing the kind of thing he wanted most to write. It was a romance, the same kind of romance he might have written ten years earlier, and not so different in theme from the romance of "Jim of the Cave." Only the setting was different. The romance was enacted against a backdrop of purple hills, vast deserts, and lonely skies.

In contrast to the scenic background of his story, the writer was living in most unglamorous conditions. Winter had come and the little cottage at Lackawaxen was appallingly cold, surrounded by drifted snow and sheets of ice. Snow piled around the doorway and blew into the house through cracks in the doors and windows. In early morning, Grey swept the snow from the floors, then waded through the drifts to gather wood, which he had to chop before building the fires for the day. Frequently he was forced to make trips on foot to the village for provender. And when his chores were done, he retired to his bare little room to write. The room was furnished with nothing but a table, a chair, and a wood stove. He pulled the table as near the stove as possible and filled page after page with laborious longhand. From time to time he paused in his writing, opened the door of the stove and held his numb fingers over the glowing coals for warmth.

When the romance was at last completed, he added a carefully handwritten title page:

THE HERITAGE OF THE DESERT

By

ZANE GREY

Then he made one more trip to New York to the publishing house on Franklin Square, up the familiar broad stairway and into the office of Ripley Hitchcock.

Placing the manuscript on the latter's desk he said, "This is the kind of book I have been wanting to write for years, and I believe it is good. I know you are convinced that I can never write fiction but I think—and I *hope*—you will change your opinion if you will only read this manuscript. I particularly want you to read it first."

Without further explanation he strode from the office. At the corner of Pearl Street he paused once more, his hand on the iron post that had steadied him after his last encounter with the publisher. Once more he went home to Lackawaxen to wait, and once more he received a letter from the House of Harper summoning him to call upon Mr. Hitchcock at his convenience.

He made all haste to New York and presented himself at the office of Mr. Hitchcock, scarcely daring to hope and totally incapable of visualizing the scene that was to follow. For Mr. Hitchcock was sitting at his desk, smiling broadly and holding out a sheet of paper, with dotted lines on it.

A half hour later Zane Grey was standing again at the Pearl Street corner, but what a difference in the scene! Instead of despair he was filled with bright hope for the future and deep gratitude for the present. The only similarity between this occasion and that of the bitterest day of his life was the mist across his eyes that blurred his vision. He was still in a daze when he arrived in Lackawaxen and made his way on snowshoes from the station to the snowbound cottage where his wife and infant son were waiting.

This was only the first of many such contracts Zane Grey was to sign with Harper and Brothers, for it was the beginning of a business relationship that was to last the rest of his life, throughout his writing career. Many years later, when the phantoms of failure and insecurity had ceased to haunt him, the author wrote:

"In the years that have come and gone, I have passed many and many a time the corner of Pearl Street where I met the crisis of my life. Never did I fail to stand a moment with my arm around that iron post. Nor was there a time when my eyes were wholly clear."

Tonto Basin

Zane Grey had a fortunate capacity for storing up vivid memories in the recesses of his mind and drawing upon them, many years later, to produce the plot or background for his writings. *The Last of the Plainsmen*, written immediately after his Western trip with Buffalo Jones, contained only a small part of his recollections of the great adventure. The remainder of the memories he filed away for future reference, unconscious that they would be used later to provide local color and settings for his novels.

Meanwhile, with the official report of the expedition off to press, he let his mind wander back to his pioneer ancestors, the Zanes, and the days of the early settlements in Ohio. Much of the material he had read preparatory to writing *Betty Zane* and *The Spirit of the Border* remained unused, but unforgotten. Gradually it took shape in his mind and he began to write his third historical novel, *The Last Trail*.

The story was woven around the romance of Helen Sheppard and Jonathan Zane, younger brother of Colonel Ebenezer Jane. Jonathan was not a mere pioneer, but a

48

"borderman," a fine distinction which the Colonel himself explained to Helen Sheppard when she inquired.

"I am a pioneer," said the Colonel. "A borderman is an Indian hunter, or scout. For years my cabins housed Andrew Zane, Sam and John McCollock, Bill Metzar, and John and Martin Wetzel, all of whom are dead. Not one saved his scalp. Fort Henry is growing; it has pioneers, rivermen, soldiers, but only two bordermen. Wetzel and Jonathan are the only ones we have left of those great men. . . . The fort there, and all these cabins, would be only black ashes, save for them, and as for us, our wives and children—God only knows."

With a woman's curiosity, Helen Sheppard asked whether the bordermen did not have wives and children of their own, to which Colonel Zane replied, "Such joys are not for bordermen. They cannot be bordermen unless free as the air blows."

It was because of Helen that Jonathan Zane gave up his life as an Indian scout and left the burden upon Lew Wetzel, the last great borderman. Although the story is packed with thrilling escapades of encounters with border renegades, of kidnapings, and of Indian massacres, and notwithstanding the fact that it revolves about the romance of Jonathan Zane, the reader finds himself waiting for the sudden and mysterious appearances of Wetzel. For Lew Wetzel, the Avenger, the Wind of Death, is the real hero of the story, as he was the hero of its author from early childhood.

None of the Zane stories was a tremendous commercial success at the time, largely because their publication was arranged by the author himself and no great publicity was ever achieved for them. All three stories became exceedingly popular years later, when the reprint rights were sold to Grosset and Dunlap of New York.

49

Of the three, *Betty Zane* has enjoyed the greatest sales and the most prolonged popularity, but *The Last Trail* displays more verve of style, more skill in narrative and characterization. The years of persistent effort had obviously enabled the writer to drop some of his self-consciousness and write more fluently, particularly when he found himself on familiar ground as he most certainly did when it was a question of family history.

Baseball, too, was familiar territory, and often in his daydreams he returned to those happy days on the diamond and to the countless episodes that make baseball history. He recalled a time when he had been responsible for losing a game to Harvard after an unusually exciting contest. Grey was playing left field for Pennsylvania, on a poorly-kept diamond which did double duty during the track season, and was badly cut up by the spiked shoes of the runners. It was in the ninth inning, with the score tied, Harvard at bat and the bases full, when the Harvard batter popped a high fly to left field. It was an easy catch. Grey was under it, his glove outstretched. He took one step forward and into a deep hole, which threw him off balance and made him miss the catch. The ball struck him on the head and bounced off into the bleachers. Harvard scored three quick runs and won the game.

To offset the memory of this tragi-comic episode from his college days was the recollection of a more fortunate incident. It was in the days of "Dutch" Carter, and Grey was playing at shortstop against Yale. There was a tense moment when the game hung in the balance. A powerful Yale batter connected with a fast ball for a sure home run. Without any hope of stopping it, Grey automatically threw out his hand—and suddenly he was aware that the ball was secure in his grip, his hand was numb, and the stands were going wild.

Musing upon the luck of the game, and the characters of the players he had known, both in college and in the leagues, he delved once more into his store of past experiences to write *The Shortstop*, a book designed primarily for boy readers. Here he had a sure-fire hit, for as the author himself observed, "Any boy loves baseball; if he doesn't, he isn't a boy."

The Shortstop, though a novel written in the third person, is autobiographical to a certain extent, for it narrates the experiences of a small-town boy who pitches a baffling curve. Chase Alloway left home to make a name for himself in baseball and, incidentally, to earn support for his mother and crippled brother. His first adventure was as a "ringer" with the Brownsville nine, when he duplicated the author's own experience of pitching a winning game against the unbeatable Jacktown Team, only to be declared a "crooked pitcher" and pursued by the angry Jacktown crowd as he fled, minus trousers, through a nearby cornfield.

The "crooked pitcher" was said to be a jinx. Bad luck followed him wherever he went, and on his tour of Ohio and Michigan looking for a spot on a professional ball team, he was spurned by superstitious managers and players until at last he was given a chance at shortstop on the Findlay team. Of course he made good with the team and with his favorite girl fan; but *The Shortstop* is more than a success story. It contains all the atmosphere of baseball: the camaraderie of the diamond, the good-natured razzing and jealous quarrels in the locker room, the excitement of winning and the heartbreak of losing, the adulation of the fans and the inconsistency of umpires. It is a defense of baseball as a clean sport, justifiably called the all-American game, and of professional ball players who, despite rough exteriors, are revealed to be open-heartedly generous and sentimental. One of the highlights of the book is the hero's defense of Sunday baseball. It was a moral issue with him, for he had been brought up to respect the Sabbath, but he concluded at last that there could be nothing wrong about a sport that brought joy to thousands of spectators who toiled from dawn to dark six days a week and had but one day free to watch the game that they had never had time or opportunity to play.

The Shortstop demonstrated that Zane Grey had a flair for writing for youth. In subsequent years he added more baseball stories to the list, all containing episodes from his own baseball career and all presenting some message or moral of sportsmanlike behavior. *The Young Pitcher,* published in 1911, was a recapitulation of Grey's baseball days in college. In the guise of Ken Ward, he re-lived his humiliating experiences as a green and unhappy freshman, homesick and friendless, innocently infringing upon upperclass territory and thereby incurring the active animosity of the sophomores.

How painful these memories were to the author is evidenced by the vividness of his description of "Ken Ward's" reactions to student life. Even the passage of years had not eradicated the recollection of feeling alone in the midst of a crowd; of the insight that made it possible for him to spot other freshmen as lonely as himself, and of the shyness that made it impossible for him to befriend them; of despairing so bitterly that there seemed no solution other than to abandon the college career; of renewed determination to fight it out rather than disappoint his father. All his bewilderment was summed up in one sentence: "Ken was not sure what

was to blame; he knew he had fallen in his own esti-
mation, and that the less he thought of himself the more
he hated the Sophs."

The turning point in Ken Ward's college life came
when he clashed with a mob of upperclassmen and held
them at bay, single-handed, by the grace of his good
pitching arm and a bag of potatoes. The potato episode
which had won Grey his position on the varsity nine at
Pennsylvania is retold as a part of the story of Ken Ward
at Wayne, so there is little doubt that the writer identified himself with Ken Ward. To make the narrative
even more personal, he introduced Reddy Ray, star of
the outfield, ace hitter, the "spark" of the team and
general guardian of Ken Ward's morale. "He was tall,
graceful, powerful, had red hair, keen dark eyes, a clean-
cut profile and square jaw." He was, in real life, none
other than "Reddy" Grey, the author's younger brother.

Reddy Ray appeared again some years later as a professional ball player in the story "The Redheaded Outfield," written originally for the McClure Newspaper
Syndicate and later published in a collection of baseball
short stories titled *The Redheaded Outfield and Other
Stories*. "Reddy Ray was a whole game in himself," according to the author's statement, an observation which
leaves no doubt as to Zane Grey's admiration for his
brother.

In all the baseball stories are incidents—comic, tragic,
and exciting—that occurred in the author's own life. The
characters, too, are drawn from his own life, even to
their exact names in some instances, as in the case of
"Tay-Tay Mohler," the stuttering fielder in "The Manager of Madden's Hill." Tay Mohler had played baseball with Grey on the McIntire Park diamond back in
Zanesville.

If it was easy for Zane Grey to wander at will back through the baseball phase of his past, it was even more easy for him to revisit the scenes of his great Western adventure. Without doubt he did this as he was writing *The Heritage of the Desert*, which was published by Harper's in 1910, and his next great Western romance, *Riders of the Purple Sage*, published in 1912. In his imagination he returned to the glamorous land of his dreams with the youthful heroes of *The Young Forester* (1910) and *The Young Lion Hunter*.

But it was not enough to return by way of the imagination or the written word. He had to return in the flesh.

In 1913, with a comfortable income from his books, particularly the two romances, he was able to finance an expedition to the great Southwest. This time he set out light-heartedly, for his wife and children were well provided for and, having proved his ability to write in a wide variety of literary forms including romances, historical novels, non-fiction narrative, and sports stories for boys, his future as a writer was assured.

At the time he embarked on his second Western expedition, *Riders of the Purple Sage* was already a best-seller, although its success had not come about without a struggle on the part of the author. Despite the growing sales of his first romance, Harper's was reluctant to publish the second one and no magazine editor would consent to serialize it, even though Grey was convinced it would be easily adaptable to serial form. He won his point with Harper's by carrying the manuscript to the vice-president, Mr. Duneka, with the special request that the latter grant him the favor of reading it himself. Both Mr. Duneka and his wife read it and liked it, which was fortunate indeed for the House of Harper. *Riders of the*

Purple Sage was published in 1912; by 1934 it had sold more than a million and a half copies and had won its author a prominent place on the list of America's most popular writers.

This did not mean that Zane Grey's business troubles were over; as he remarked many years later: "They never have been." Business details were always irksome to him. His wife assumed the major part of this burden, leaving him free to write and to travel as he saw fit. But with the care of an active little boy, and a new little girl, named Betty Zane, Mrs. Grey could not give as much time to her task of self-appointed business manager for her husband. He had to spend more and more time conferring with editors and publishers, who did not always agree with him. These sessions left him weary and full of a longing to escape to a simpler life where man battles, not against other men, but against the elements.

His escape in 1913 was well planned. He had heard of John Wetherill, the discoverer of "Nonnezoshe," the canyon of the Rainbow Bridge in Utah, and had written to Wetherill inducing him to serve as his guide on an expedition into this strange new country. Theirs was only the second non-scientific expedition to be made into the Rainbow Bridge canyon; Theodore Roosevelt and a party of his friends made the trip some years later, also under the guidance of John Wetherill.

Grey was not disappointed. With Wetherill and his Navajo guides, he rode through Monument Valley "and the mysterious and labyrinthine Canyon Segi," rich in Indian legend, unbelievable in natural beauty. Grey's eager eyes photographed each scene, to be treasured in retrospect after his return to the tedium of routine life. Not a detail missed his attention; every wild desert flower was noted and its name learned. Every day was an adventure in itself.

After many hairbreadth escapes and days of climbing the treacherous, serpentine mountain trails with their pack horses, they came in sight of the natural Rainbow Bridge, named by the Indians for its many changing hues. The party pitched camp in the shadow of the Bridge, and Grey observed its vicissitudes with the changing lights of day. He described it in *Tales of Lonely Trails*, a book that was not published until 1922, with the clarity of a scientist and the appreciation of a poet: "a rosy-hued, tremendous arch of stone," "a rainbow magnified even beyond dreams," "a work of ages, sweeping up majestically from the red walls, its iris-hued arch against the blue sky," "black and mystic at night, transparent and rosy in the sunrise, and at sunset a flaming curve limned against the heavens."

Refreshed by this contact with nature, the author turned homeward and buried himself in work. His next two romances of the West, *Desert Gold* and *The Light of Western Stars*, were soon off to the publishers and, incidentally, were eagerly accepted as magazine serials.

But from that time forward, his dreams of the lonely places that fascinated him were no longer idle dreams. They became specific plans for the greatly-anticipated trips he could take between novels. Variety and change were necessary to the writer's happiness; they were necessary to his continued success as a writer. So he became something of a vagabond during a few months of each year, exploring hidden trails and hunting in unknown forests of the West, trout-fishing in mountain streams, game-fishing off the coasts of Florida, Cuba, and California, penetrating the wilds of Mexico and Yucatan, crossing the desert wastelands that held almost a mystic fascination for him.

Often he was accompanied on these trips by his brother, "Reddy," who became known to the readers of Zane Grey's non-fiction narratives simply as "R.C." There was a great affinity between the two brothers. They understood each other's moods, they liked the same things, and they enjoyed a friendly spirit of rivalry in their sportsmanship. R.C., who acted as his brother's secretary for a number of years, was the more realistic of the pair and not given so much to temperament. His was an exuberant, enthusiastic nature as a rule, and it fell to him to encourage Zane in days of luckless fishing as in days of tiresome writing. He was not as daring as his famous brother, but in Zane's eyes he was as great a woodsman and fisherman as he was a baseball player, and in the accounts of their expeditions together are frequent admiring references to the prowess of R.C., "who could handle an axe as he used to swing a baseball bat."

Together they fished in the lagoons of Florida and the mountain streams of Oregon. They hunted bear and elk in Colorado. Spending their summers at Avalon, the angler's paradise, they fished for tuna and broadbill swordfish off the California coast. And in 1918 they took young Romer Grey, then a lad of nine, on his first trip into the wilds of the Tonto Basin in Arizona. The boy proved to his father's satisfaction that "he was a Zane, all right," and the two men watched his reactions with considerable amusement and a bit of inevitable nostalgia for their own boyhood. With some consternation they observed his lust for the kill and his primitive joy at shooting his first squirrel. His elders, seasoned hunters as they were, cringed at the thought of killing so harmless and friendly a creature as a squirrel, but when they recalled similar scenes from their own past when killing was an object in itself, they knew they were in no position to reprimand him.

"Doesn't he remind you of ourselves when we were his age?" R.C. mused aloud, and Zane reflected soberly that "boys are blood-thirsty little savages."

Romer may have been slightly more blood-thirsty than other boys his age, for in spite of everything teachers and parents had done to deter him, he had managed to read all of his father's books, and had re-read all the "blood-and-thunder" passages that would have made an adult reader's blood run cold. These he could quote verbatim at the drop of a hat. Among fictitious characters, his preference ran to outlaws and gunmen. Among real characters, his idols were his father and Lew Wetzel. He was extremely proud of his Zane ancestry and particularly of the trace of Indian blood that flowed in their veins. Zane Grey was certain he saw manifestations of that Indian heritage in the younger generation as he watched his son creeping stealthily through the brush stalking wild turkey, or on his hands and knees examining bear tracks.

It was a thrilling experience for the boy. They moved from one campsite to another, following their own inclinations and the trail of fresh game. Days were spent in fishing or hunting turkey, grouse, deer, and bear. When evening came they gathered around the campfire, filling their empty stomachs, swapping yarns with other hunters they encountered and listening to the tales of the Navajos. They slept on soft pine-needles under the stars, and never has a boy slept more soundly than did young Romer Grey on those nights. He was so eager to prove himself that he would never admit his fatigue, but the men were quick to observe the signs and to call for rest, or even, over violent protests, force the boy to remain in camp for a day while they pursued the hunt.

It was on one of those rare occasions that Zane Grey met a cinnamon bear in a face-to-face encounter he never forgot. Leaving Romer in camp, he and R.C. set off on a bear-hunt one morning and in the course of the day became separated while making their way through dense timber. While Zane was seeking to rejoin his brother, his horse became frightened, obviously by the scent of bear, and bolted. The horse was difficult to manage, but the thick underbrush was even more so and it was no reflection upon Grey's horsemanship that he was left draped on the bough of a scraggly juniper. From the sound of crashing brush, it appeared that the juniper was in the direct path of the bear. Following the direction of the sound, he could see the animal's cinnamon coat gleaming through the close-woven leaves. From his precarious perch, he took aim and fired. The bear, if hit at all, was only angered by the shot and continued to crash through the brush toward the juniper, from which the terrified hunter had fallen as he fired the gun. He aimed again into the crackling brush but in vain; his gun had jammed.

There was nothing to do but find a sturdier tree—and run for it. This he did, and scampered up the straight trunk as nimbly as a squirrel. From his new and safer perch he watched the inexorable advance of the wild beast as it approached the edge of the clearing. Suddenly it emerged from the brush only a few yards away—but something was wrong with the picture. This bear had horns! The hunter was too astonished to be amused when the brown steer broke through into the clearing, blinked in the sunlight, and then—untouched by bullet and unmindful of human presence—ambled leisurely toward the trail.

Back in camp he soon forgot his embarrassment as well as the cuts and bruises and stiff muscles he had incurred as a result of his extraordinary exertion in escaping a make-believe foe. In his absence news had reached camp of the great influenza epidemic. It was raging through the Indian reservation nearby and, according to the Navajos, no one could escape it. It was sweeping the entire country.

Somberly they broke camp. The men were fearful not only for the welfare of their hunting party but for their families, who were then residing in California. Romer's first hunting trip was at an end. They made all haste to Flagstaff, and thence to Los Angeles where they were relieved to find that all was well with the Grey family.

Thereupon Grey's mood of depression over the abrupt conclusion of his expedition vanished and he became immersed once more in plans for the next year's outing. For with characteristic optimism, when he and R.C. had parted company with their friends and guides, they had agreed to meet Copple, Lee and Al Doyle, and the two Haight brothers in that same spot, at twelve o'clock noon of September 21st of the following year.

At it turned out, Grey was four and one-half hours late in keeping that appointment. In the fall of 1919, his usually rugged health failed him and he approached the wilderness rendezvous sick in body and spirit, with none of the zest that had characterized his anticipation of the trip the preceding year. A part of the trouble—possibly a larger part than he imagined—lay in the absence of Romer, for they had become great companions and it was with difficulty that he had persuaded the boy to remain in school so that he could better afford to stay out later to go on the African game hunt they had planned together. Zane was almost sorry he had not permitted the boy to accompany them, for he missed him very much. Even the reassurances of R.C., the cheery presence of their Japanese cook, Takahashi, as well as the pleasant comradeship of the other participants of the hunt, failed to cheer him.

From the description of his malady—the burning fever, the aching muscles and joints. the great inertia that pervaded his body—it is highly probable that Grey was himself a victim of influenza without knowing it. And even if he had known the extent of his illness it is doubtful if he would ever have admitted it. For he scorned human weakness and exalted, almost above all other traits, man's physical strength and endurance. The trip might have been a total loss as far as he was concerned had it not provided him with an excellent opportunity to prove his pet theory that bodily ills are best cured by the rigors of a strenuous life in the open, rather than by pills and pampering.

He went to great lengths to prove the theory, with a treatment so drastic that it was bound either to kill or to cure. He forced himself to ride when he was too weak to mount a horse without first climbing up on a rock. The long ride from Flagstaff, accompanied by the Doyles who had previously served as guides for him, together with R.C., Takahashi, and his friend Nielsen, to the campsite where they were to meet the rest of their party, was the most laborious journey he had ever made in his life, and he was forced to stop at intervals and stretch his aching bones, lying flat on his back, convinced that he would never be able to move again. But each time he arose and continued doggedly on the trail. It was because of these enforced rests that he did not arrive at the rendezvous at the appointed hour and lost his reputation for punctuality, a point that irritated him considerably.

Once arrived at the camp, he slept through the night, but was up at dawn to continue his self-inflicted treatment. He hauled logs in to camp, spent hours chopping wood for the campfire, and engaged in all conceivable forms of exercise to test his strength and fit him for the expedition ahead. By the first of October, the opening day of the hunting season, he was in good enough condition to go into the woods with his fellows and join in the hunt.

All the while, he seemed to be there in body but not in spirit. "I did not awaken to the old zest and thrill of the open," he recorded. "Something was wrong with me."

This is not to say that he did not enjoy the expedition. He did. But on this occasion he found his enjoyment in different things, being more impressed with the quiet pleasures of solitude or the comradeship of the camp than in the excitement of the hunt. His account of the trip, published in the collection of *Tales of Lonely Trails*, bears a more pensive and philosophical note than is characteristic of his earlier writings.

He was tremendously impressed by the cheerful Takahashi, who was himself something of a philosopher. The cook went about his work with quiet good-humor, kept the camp neat, chopped firewood, and took pride in planning tempting menus for the hunters. He had a supply of popcorn with him and often popped large quantities of it over the open fire at night. It was with a gentle amusement that the author recalled Takahashi's soliloquy on popcorn: "You eat all time—much popcorn—just so long you keep mouth going all same like horse—you happy." He was amused, too—as was the rest of the party—over Takahashi's innocent capture of the pretty little animal that turned out to be a skunk, and a treacherous one at that.

But possibly what impressed him most about the Oriental was his cheerful acceptance of the world he lived in, and his simple contentment. It may have been the contrast of Takahashi that caused Grey to write critically of himself: "I can never do anything reasonably. I always overdo everything. But what happiness I derive from anticipation! When I am not working, I live in dreams, partly of the past, but mostly of the future. A man should live only in the present."

In the Jungles of Mexico

Zane Grey's first taste of Western life during the Buffalo Jones expedition had filled him with new ideas and a determination to revisit the scene of this initial adventure in outdoor life. Another expedition which left an equally strong impression with him was his first experience with tarpon fishing at Tampico. The memory of this adventure bore with it the visual image of an incredibly beautiful mountain cascade he had glimpsed from the train window en route to his destination in southeastern Mexico.

"The first fall was a long white streak," he recalled, "ending in a dark pool; below came cascade after cascade, fall after fall, some wide, others narrow, and all white and green against the yellow rock. Then the train curved round a spur of the mountain, descended to a level, to be lost in a luxuriance of jungle growth."

These were the Micas Falls, he learned, forming a part of the mysterious Santa Rosa River. No map of Mexico indicated the river's course, nor did any of the natives seem to know its source, but all were agreed that it was filled with beautiful and dangerous rapids and that it probably flowed into the Panuco River.

The vague surmises of the natives were unsatisfactory to Zane Grey's inquisitive mind, and their warnings of jungle hazards served only as a challenge. He was determined to learn for himself the secrets of the unknown river.

Three years passed before he was able to return and keep his rendezvous with the Santa Rosa. When he did, he heard repeated warnings, and more specific ones, of the risks involved in what the natives considered a wild goose chase. There were alligators and crocodiles; wild pigs and fierce tigers; venomous snakes and deadly insects.

All this did not deter him, and he set about to find a companion to accompany him on the trip. He spent a few days fishing for tarpon and talked to many of the international sporting set gathered there for the fishing season. When he mentioned his plan to them, he found that they reacted even more strongly than did the natives. At last he chanced to meet George Allen, a young American who had been in Tampico for two years as an employee of a railroad company. Allen was due for a vacation and was enthusiastic over the prospects of exploring the Santa Rosa.

Common sense told Grey that the boy was extremely young and inexperienced for such a venture, but intuition told him that Allen's enthusiasm and spirit of adventure were assets not to be overlooked. Perhaps when he made his decision he was recalling his own youthful pleas addressed to Buffalo Jones, and his gratitude to the older man who had given him his first chance. At any rate, he agreed to take Allen with him, and together they began to accumulate the requisite equipment, first of which was a boat.

A boatman was essential to the expedition, and the

two would-be explorers cast about for likely prospects. Here again the Grey intuition came to the fore in the selection of Pepe, a Mexican guide who had served him on previous excursions. Since their last meeting, however, Pepe had retrograded. Allen reported that Pepe had been one of the best boatmen on the river until he suffered loss of reputation by reason of excessive drinking. He did, indeed, look much the worse for wear, ill-clad and unkempt. Grey knew that if ever a man needed a job, Pepe did; yet pride would not permit him to beg for work—pride or the conviction that no one would ever want to hire him again.

One glance at the human derelict with his tattered clothing, lacklustre eyes, and apathetic manner should have convinced anyone that he was not the man to face the rugged life of the jungle. But the mere sight of the man aroused Zane Grey's sympathies—and besides, there were rumors that Pepe's wife and children were in dire need. When he offered Pepe a job at three pesos a day—three times the amount ordinarily paid to *mozos*—the poor man nearly collapsed.

It was strictly an act of charity, though Grey would never admit it. He preferred to justify his judgment by claiming that he was playing a hunch. "I conceived a liking for Pepe," he explained, "and believed I could trust him. Besides, in hiring guides or choosing companions for a wild adventure, I had learned to trust to an inexplicable impulse."

Fishermen along the river repeated the tale of the gringo who had been foolish enough to give Pepe a job, and trusting enough to give him money in advance to buy new clothing and equipment. The money, they said, would be lost in liquor, and the gringo would never see Pepe again.

Time proved that they were wrong and that Grey's intuition had not led him astray. Pepe reported to him at the appointed time, resplendent in new jacket and trousers, with a brilliant sash at his waist. His feet, which had been bare when Grey first accosted him, were now shod in good sturdy boots. His face, though still bearing the haggard lines left by the hard life he had led, was clean and shaven, and there was a look of pride in his eye as he displayed the equipment he had bought for the journey. Grey noted with great satisfaction that the man had made prudent purchases, and it was a source of pride to him to observe the new respect on the faces of the *mozos* who had predicted no good end for Pepe.

"What a little thing," the author mused, "will win back a man's hope and self-respect."

Pepe entered into the final preparations as enthusiastically as young Allen. Grey himself was excited, but with characteristic thoroughness, he paid careful attention to the minutest details of shopping and packing.

Distrustful of canoes in swift waters, he had succeeded in finding a light, flat-bottomed boat that suited their purpose admirably, and into it they packed all the provisions they would need for several weeks: food supplies, cooking utensils, blankets, canvas tenting, rope, axes, and firearms. Perishables had to be waterproofed; guns and ammunition and cameras had to be easily accessible but protected from water damage; and the boat needed to be packed in such a way as to provide flat surfaces for sitting without making the load topheavy.

When the boat was all packed, the three adventurers entrained for Valles, the small station near which the railroad bridge crossed the Santa Rosa. Here they spent the night, waiting for their equipment which was following by freight.

Foreigners were seldom seen in the tiny village of Valles, and its inhabitants took great interest in the party. When they learned of the proposed trip into the jungle, their friendly concern gave way to genuine alarm and they pleaded with the explorers to abandon their wild plan before harm should befall them. Their consternation became more understandable to Allen and Grey when their boat was unloaded from the morning freight. The natives viewed it with a mingling of astonishment and fear that indicated clearly they had never before seen a boat. The adventurous Americans experienced a moment of doubt themselves as they realized they were about to embark on a trek down a river where boats were unknown. But after a brief moment of wonder at the foolhardiness of their venture, they continued preparations with as much zest as ever.

A mule-cart had to be engaged to haul the boat down the narrow trail to the river's edge, and villagers crowded about to watch the strange proceedings. Their excitement over the event presaged the adventures that awaited the travelers.

That night, encamped at the water's edge and prepared to embark at early dawn, they had a preview of the abundance and variety of wild life to be encountered in the Mexican jungle. There were ducks in large flocks, Mexican turkey, pheasant, quail, songbirds whose melodies were familiar to the Americans, and hordes of screeching parrots whose discordant clamor drowned the voices of the songsters.

After a hurried breakfast, camp was broken and the expedition got under way. The plan was to go upriver to Micas Falls the first day, then to retrace their way on the second day and proceed on downstream to the point

where the Santa Rosa flowed, presumably, into the Panuco—a distance which Grey estimated at 175 miles.

Intent as he was upon reaching the long-remembered
Micas Falls, Grey soon became absorbed in the jungle
scenery as Pepe plied the oars. Bird life was even more
plentiful along the sheltered river bank than the morning chorus of birds would have led him to believe. He
noted the exotic coloring and markings of tropical birds
he had never seen before, as well as the familiar pheasants,
bitterns, herons, cranes, and kingfishers. He was enchanted by the jungle foliage: mossy cypress, trailing
vines, clumps of bamboo, graceful palms, and gray-
barked cebia covered with orchids. Occasionally, a writh-
ing, slithering movement in the trees reminded him of
the hidden dangers underlying the deceptively serene
surface of the setting, and he recalled the words of
hunters who had claimed to have seen snakes twenty
feet long, with bodies as large around as a man's leg.

He turned his attention to the less alarming aspects
of tiger-cats slipping stealthily through the dense under-
growth, and the myriads of animals, including a band of
some thirty-odd ringtailed raccoons, who came to their
accustomed watering places at the river's edge.

Meanwhile, Pepe was supplying the Mexican names of
the strange birds and animals, and making comments on
their surroundings, with George Allen acting as interpreter. Allen himself was mainly interested in the hunting opportunities and in his enthusiasm would have killed
enough game for a caravan if Grey had not admonished
him to shoot only what they needed for food.

Hunting and nature-lore were both forgotten, however, when a rumbling sound warned of rapids ahead. The
deep channel of the Santa Rosa became suddenly shallow
and rowing was impossible. The men pushed the boat

along through the shallow rapids, wading in water only knee-deep in some places. Before reaching the top of the rapid, they encountered the first real hazard of the trip, in the shape of an eight-foot alligator which Pepe struck with his oar.

From then on, great caution was exercised whenever wading was necessary, as it frequently was, for there were eighteen rapids to traverse within an estimated distance of ten miles, each rapid becoming progressively rougher as they ascended the river. Then the river narrowed and deepened again as they approached the first real waterfall.

Here the boat had to be lifted up by ropes and, after a great deal of strenuous pulling and hauling, the weary travelers were rewarded only by the sight of yet another treacherous rapid and a series of waterfalls, like stair-steps in the river. Progress thereafter was so slow that the plan to attain Micas Falls by dusk was abandoned. A good campsite was found on a grassy bank overlooking the stream, and while Pepe and George unloaded equipment Grey set out alone to inspect the terrain.

There were evidences here of forest fire, which explained the sparseness of jungle foliage and the absence of birds at this point. The mountains were nearby, and in the stillness he could hear the echo of a train winding along the mountain slope. Then he caught a glimpse of the Micas Falls, as magnificent as they had appeared to him when he first sighted them three years earlier.

Although the heat was intense and the ascent to the falls was difficult, Grey could not miss the opportunity for a closer view. Returning to camp, he got his camera and set out on the steep upward climb. From the foot of the falls, the view reminded him of "a series of green fans, strung together with silver ribbon." He remained beside the falls to watch the sun set behind the blue mountains.

On the downward climb he surprised a herd of deer, so tame that it was obvious no hunters had penetrated this area previously. Grey felt an instant's regret that he had left his rifle in camp, but when he reflected that George had provided enough wild fowl for a feast, he was glad to let the creatures go unmolested.

When he returned to camp, he found that he had unwittingly captured a goodly supply of wild life on his shirt.

"*Pinilius!*" Pepe exclaimed, seeming to derive some amusement from the sight of the countless little red specks clinging to his leader's shirt.

The battle of the ticks began. Grey found that the ticks had no inclination to bite him, though they clung to his clothing like grim death and had to be removed forcibly, one by one. While he was engaged in this never-ending task, George and Pepe were cutting brush and building a campfire. Coming in with armloads of firewood, they found themselves covered with *pinilius* and the larger, fiercer *garrapatas*.

Even the *garrapatas* had no taste for Grey, but they fed eagerly upon his two companions, who periodically emitted howls of rage and pain. As soon as the fire was blazing, they seated themselves in the circle of light and went to work on their tormentors with lighted cigarettes.

Grey, who was not a smoker, moved closer to see what they were doing. Methodically and without the faintest touch of humor, they were pursuing the ticks with the glowing ends of cigarettes. George had crossed one leg over the other and was making rhythmic stabs at the bared flesh with his cigarette tip.

"What on earth are you doing?" Grey demanded.

"Popping ticks," George replied laconically.

Looking over his shoulder, Grey saw the effect of the burning cigarette. When held within a quarter of an inch of the insect, it produced a resounding "Pop!" as *pinilius* or *garrapata* exploded in midair from the intensity of the heat.

Amazement gave way to amusement as Grey, still unbitten, watched his comrades go about their deadly pursuit in deep earnestness. Choking with laughter, he listened to the steady "pop-pop-pop" of dying ticks. He could even detect the difference between the pop of the little *pinilius* and the louder pop of the *garrapatas* who, according to Pepe, were "mothers of the *pinilius*."

It was Pepe who was bothered most by the tiny *pinilius*, while the *garrapatas* showed a distinct preference for George. When that discovery was made, Grey gave his companions the nicknames that stuck with them throughout the trip: Garrapato George and Pinilius Pepe.

George, vengefully pledging sudden and violent death to any *garrapata* that dared to bite him, found nothing amusing in his new nickname. "Just wait," he predicted darkly. "You'll be popping ticks yourself before you see Tampico again."

Grey reflected that the boy was probably right, but he did all in his power to preclude the possibility on the spot. With flaming torches made from dead palm branches, he singed the grass and brush around the campsite, popping ticks on a larger scale than George or Pepe had ever contemplated. The treatment was effective and, after a hearty meal, the men crawled into their tent for a peaceful night's rest.

In the middle of the night the jungle silence was shattered by an ear-splitting yell. Grey had his hand on his revolver before he was fully awake. Bright moonlight illumined the scene. George was sitting up on his blankets, blinking sleepily. Beyond him, Pepe's place under the canvas was vacant.

In front of the tent the Mexican stood clawing at his clothing like a madman and babbling a torrent of Spanish invective unintelligible even to George, all the while pointing down at the ground. The cause of the uproar was soon apparent. Their tent was being invaded by an army of black jungle ants, moving as was their custom in a straight line, regardless of obstacles. Pepe being just one more obstacle to surmount, they had swarmed over him and, when he moved, had bitten him thoroughly.

While Pepe brushed ants from his body, the remaining army closed ranks and marched on—a solid stream of black, measuring a foot in width and of sufficient length that, even though it marched rapidly, it required a full hour to cross the other two beds and move on out of the tent.

Their sleep thus disturbed, the men slept late the next morning, until the screeching of parrots awakened them. Breakfast over, they broke camp and started on their trip downstream, for Grey had decided there was no point in attempting to approach any nearer to Micas Falls by boat, especially since he had already viewed the falls at close range.

Grey took the oars from Pepe, for he was more experienced with swift mountain streams, and through his skillful maneuvering they were able to shoot most of the rapids, resorting to wading and pulling only at the worst of the falls. Pepe had been somewhat wounded when asked to relinquish the oars, but after several hours of travel he admiringly proclaimed Grey a master boatman.

The boat handled like a dream and all went well despite George's dire predictions that the ants' nocturnal invasion of their tent would prove an evil omen for the day. His warnings were borne out with a suddenness that left him more bewildered than the others.

At a point where the river curved sinuously and the rapids ran in swift, deep channels, Grey resisted the temptation to test his boating skill and decided to tow the boat through along the shoreline. The plan was a wise one but Pepe, misunderstanding a command spoken in English, pulled the boat in too near the shore, pinning Grey in a helpless position against the bank. Meanwhile George, forgetful of his duties as interpreter, stood at the water's edge firing shot after shot at a herd of deer he had spotted farther downstream.

George missed the deer and then turned to shout excited commands at Pepe who, in his confusion, dropped the tow rope and let the boat go careening into the swift main current. Without hesitation, Pepe dived in after it, and to his watching companions it appeared for several anxious moments that both he and the boat were lost.

But Pepe succeeded in recovering his grip on the rope and though tossed and buffeted by the churning waters, escaped without injury. The boat had been out of hand long enough to fill with water, and it sank to the bottom at the rocky edge of the stream, bearing with it all the guns, ammunition, and precious photographic equipment as well as other perishables.

It took some time to salvage the boat and spread the wet cargo out in the sun to dry. Camera and film, fortunately, were not ruined, and ammunition was waterproof, but the guns had to be disassembled, cleaned, dried, and oiled. While the hot sun finished the drying process, Grey addressed his comrades severely, calling Pepe to task for losing his head and George for neglecting his share of the work in the excitement of the kill.

Both took the scolding to heart, but George was already sufficiently chastened by the discovery that his whole supply of cigarettes had been ruined by water.

Considerably sobered by the experience, the party proceeded downstream. George recovered his youthful spirits very quickly and whenever the boat was traversing the calm level stretches between rapids, he was shooting at whatever game appeared along the stream. Grey preferred to photograph the scenery, thankful that his camera had been spared.

Pepe took his turn at the oars except when the rumbling current warned of rapids ahead. Once he spotted an iguana—a giant lizard, with the general appearance of a miniature dragon—sunning himself on the rocks of a little island. Plunging from the boat, he pursued the reptile with his *machete*, but succeeded only in chopping off its tail without preventing its retreat into the thicket. Pepe returned to the boat covered with *pinilius* and filled with chagrin over the iguana's escape. He had planned to make a feast of the tender iguana meat.

Shortly afterward, they passed under the railroad bridge and past the site of their first camp, where the villagers had gathered to watch them embark on their foolhardy venture. Beyond that, around a sharp bend in the river, was the unknown.

The water became more shallow, so that rowing was largely impossible. This meant more wading, and after jumping into and out of the boat a number of times, Grey conceived the idea of hanging his feet over the bow and guiding the boat through the rapids by an occasional kick at the shallow bottom. Pepe was quick to follow suit so that, with one man to kick from each side of the boat, it was easy to keep her course straight, although it struck them both as being a crude piece of boatsmanship.

The shallow water abounded in fish, mainly a variety of bass which Grey had never seen before and which he found difficult to catch. George tried shooting at them just to see them jump out of the water. This provided good sport until larger game appeared at the water's edge: a splendid lone deer, standing on a rocky ledge some 250 yards downstream. Handicapped by the distance and the motion of the boat, Grey had almost given up when his sixth shot went home and the deer toppled from the high promontory to fall with a resounding smack on the rocks below.

Pulling the boat in toward the rocks, they found that the deer's carcass was too badly crushed by the fall to provide more than one good slab of meat for their dinner. They carved off one haunch and left the rest for the buzzards that appeared from nowhere.

This lap of the journey would have been an easy one except for the stifling heat. For miles the river was shut in between walls of bare rock that reflected the direct rays of the sun and made the heat almost unbearable. The adventurers were scalded by the steam that arose in clouds from their wet clothing and their throats were parched with thirst. Prudently, Grey had provided quinine and anti-malaria dosages and insisted on boiling the drinking water. When their canteens were empty, Pepe drank from the river, and Grey had to forbid George to follow this example, knowing as he did that Pepe, like most native Mexicans, was endowed with a natural immunity to tropical diseases which he and George did not possess. They had to content themselves with the juice of a lime, which gave their dry throats temporary relief.

What beauty the scenery possessed was wasted on eyes

aching and bloodshot from the glaring sun. Even the thought of pitching camp and resting held little appeal when the only available campsites were bare, burning rocks. Just as a man surrounded by miles of desert becomes obsessed with the vision of water, so the sun-baked travelers became obsessed with the vision of the cool green jungle.

And there, around a bend in the river, was the longed-for sight, and with it came the first cooling breeze of evening.

They pitched camp in a grassy spot, miraculously free from ticks, and were cooking venison when Pepe sang out:

"Tiger-cats!"

Supper was forgotten in the mad rush for guns and ammunition. When the men returned to the campfire some time later, they found their supper partially burned, but they were triumphant over bagging a beautiful spotted "tiger-cat," similar to wildcats Grey had seen in the Western states, but larger and with a more valuable pelt.

Next morning deer appeared near the camp but, frightened by the first gunshot, escaped into the brush. Later, as the boat bore the party through the quiet deep waters enclosed by jungle, there was an abundance of water-fowl to keep George busy with his rifle. In these densely sheltered passages, black squirrels scampered about through the trees without fear of human invaders; ducks and herons did not even fly up at the crack of a rifle, for obviously no one had ever shot at them before.

A distant roar warned of heavy waterfalls below, and Pepe mutely handed the oars over to Grey, who had begun to have visions of a high waterfall through a gorge so narrow that portage would be impossible. Mooring the boat at a distance above the falls, they walked for a distance to ascertain the situation. The fall was not more than twelve feet high and portage, though rendered difficult by the uneven footing over jagged rocks, was not impossible. The perturbing factor, however, was the discovery that the water below the falls was foamy white as far as the eye could see, and there was an audible roaring farther downstream, distinct from the sound of the falls.

Grey knew that the rapids must be filled with rocks, and that the water was dangerously shallow. One rock could easily split their light craft asunder and leave them stranded, without transportation or equipment, miles from civilization. But if the expedition was to continue, he had to risk the rapids.

Tense with anxiety, he gripped the oars and backed the boat into the stream and felt the irresistible pull of the swift current. He was conscious that he was not handling the boat well at all, and that the lashing waves had more control over the craft than he did. The banks of the stream were nothing but a blur to his eyes as they sped down the rapids, grazing huge rocks in midstream, shooting around sharp curves without knowing what hazards lay beyond.

Just as the foot of the rapid was in sight, with calmer waters ahead, Pepe stood up and yelled. He was calling attention to a huge rock that lay directly in the boat's path, and so nearby that Grey had to plunge the oars quickly into the water. The suddenness of the jerk unbalanced Pepe and he was flung from the stern into the current.

Fortunately for Pepe, he swam like a fish, and before his comrades could rescue him, he had reached smooth water and then dry land. Terrifying as the experience

78

had been, everyone joined in the laugh as Pepe stood on the rocks shaking the water from his clothing like a wet puppy. The comedy relief was just what they needed as an antidote for high-keyed nerves. It dawned upon Grey in that moment that he had been taking his responsibilities too seriously, probably to compensate for the recklessness of the other two. But now he realized that there was such a thing as an overdose of caution, which can serve to impair efficiency and at the same time throw a wet blanket on an otherwise gay adventure. Taking his cue from the prevailing mood that followed this near-disaster, he determined to continue the trip in a spirit of devil-may-care and come-what-may.

It was well that he did. As soon as they launched out on the next lap they were hurled into a breathtaking series of rapids, swifter and more rock-infested than the ones just passed. So numerous were the rapids that Grey, concentrating on the arduous task of keeping the boat upright and missing the rocks that lay in their path, actually lost count, an amazing fact in view of his extraordinary passion for accuracy and detail.

While he was trying to estimate the number of rapids and the distance covered, they came upon a rocky bluff which appeared to be an island, for the river forked and flowed on either side, but the island—if such it was—had to be one of unusual length, for the opposite end of it could not be seen even from a high point on the rocks overhanging the water.

It was easy to decide which branch of the river to take. To the right, the water was sluggish, almost stagnant; to the left, the water flowed in greater volume and at a rapid rate, broken by shallow falls that would be quick and easy to navigate. The party voted to take the left branch, and were soon reveling in the excitement of shooting the rapids at breakneck speed. Grey developed a technique that added fun to the game and saved time on the way. As they approached a shallow fall, he would drop off the bow, hold the boat back and swing it straight, then jump back in just before the boat plunged over the drop. He repeated this trick so many times that it became almost routine—until he underestimated a fall and found that he was holding the boat at the brink of a four-foot drop.

George and Pepe, sitting in the stern, were unaware of the danger, nor could they grasp the situation when Grey suddenly shouted out to them: "Jump!" The stern was already shoving over the brink and Grey was pulling back desperately.

"Jump!" he roared again. "Quick, idiots!"

Only vaguely comprehending, the two automatically dived into the foaming water below the fall, and just in the nick of time, for the boat tugged away from Grey's grasp and over it went, smoothly and easily, without shipping enough water to damage any of the cargo. If the two passengers had remained aboard a second longer, the boat undoubtedly would have swamped.

The next few falls were approached more prudently, with Grey guiding the boat to the edge and the other two catching it from below. At the last of these falls, they passed on into a narrow channel sheltered on both sides by dense jungle.

It was a peaceful scene. The water was quiet and smooth, and as they drifted leisurely along, Grey had time to contemplate the beauty of the surrounding foliage and the strange silence of this wild country, without even the song of a bird reaching his ears. Lost in thought and gazing dreamily upward at the trailing moss, he was startled by a shout from Pepe:

"Santa Maria!"

The boat, at that instant, struck a mud flat. Beyond not the least trickle of water was to be seen. They had taken the branch of the river that led to a dead end. Stoically, Pepe took over the oars and started to row back upstream.

The prospect of retracing their route, up innumerable falls to the fork in the river, was almost unbearable. George was plunged in melancholy, and Grey searched his brain for an explanation as to what could have happened to the tremendous volume of swift-flowing water that had borne them so rapidly. For it to dissipate so suddenly was inconceivable, nor could he persuade himself of the possibility of a subterranean passage. He knew he had been mistaken in judging the long strip of land to be an island, but surely he could not have been wrong in assuming that the sluggish waters of the right fork held small promise for explorers. There was only one answer: somewhere was an outlet, hidden perhaps by the dense jungle foliage, that they had overlooked.

He told Pepe to row close to the bank of what they had assumed to be the island, under overhanging branches that frequently concealed the water's edge like a heavy green screen. "Low bridge!" George would sing out from time to time, and the men would flatten themselves out in the boat in order to pass under the barricade. Often Pepe had to use his machete to carve out a path for the boat.

"I hear running water!" Grey exclaimed suddenly.

Near at hand was the passage they had been seeking, hidden completely by a wall of matted vines. It took more heavy work with the machete to reveal to them the narrow, dark passage of water, canopied over by trees so thickly leaved that scarcely a ray of sunlight came through.

They drifted along with the current, unable to use the oars without scraping the bank on either side of the stream. Suddenly the current became perceptibly swifter, a light appeared at the end of the dim tunnel, and they passed into bright sunlight that dazzled their unaccustomed eyes. Ahead lay a series of steep drops over rocky ledges where the water ran too shallow for rowing.

The prospect of making another portage over uneven rocks was rendered even more distasteful on closer inspection of the banks of the stream. Sunning themselves on the rocks were countless snakes, of a variety unfamiliar to Grey, but undoubtedly a kind of water moccasin, for they glided quickly into the water when a noise startled them. Grey and his companions shrank at the thought of wading through those snake-infested waters—but it had to be done if they were to proceed.

Picking their way carefully through the shallow waters, they beached the boat and Grey went ahead through the forest to see what lay at the foot of the falls. Even before he had cleared his way through the brush, he heard the roar of rapids, and he was overjoyed when a few minutes later he found a clearing in the trees, beyond which he could see the main stream of the river.

He hurried back to tell his comrades the good news, and their relief was so great that the task of carrying their equipment around the falls was a welcome one. Several trips had to be made before the boat could be carried down the steep, narrow trail to the foot of the falls. At last they were ready for the final trip, and Grey hurried back to the boat where Pepe was rearranging the remainder of the load.

While he was still several yards down the trail, he heard Pepe's terrified shout. He quickened his pace to a run, and George, who had been following just behind him, had caught up by the time they reached the clearing. There stood Pepe, paralyzed with fear, and pointing upward at the limb of a tree.

"Holy smoke!" George breathed.

Hanging from the limb was an enormous black snake —not at all similar to the short, brown snakes that had been seen along the water's edge, but measuring at least ten feet in length and possibly five inches in diameter. Grey did not need to recall the snake stories he had heard in Tampico to know that this was a dangerous reptile, for Pepe's babbling Spanish and bulging eyes told the story accurately enough.

George was reaching for his rifle when Grey, whose guns had already been carried downstream, stopped him. "You'll never hit him with a rifle, George. Get your shotgun."

Precious moments were wasted while George unpacked his sixteen-gauge, only to discover that a shell was jammed in the chamber and would not eject. Meanwhile the snake, swaying slowly to and fro, was watching his human foes below with deadly eyes.

Without a word, George handed his .32 to Grey.

The swaying mark presented a difficult target, and the first two shots missed the snake's head narrowly. When the head began to dart about too rapidly to draw a bead on it, Grey yielded to the temptation to send a bullet through the thick body. He knew, even as he squeezed the trigger, that it was a foolish thing to do.

Like a flash, the snake darted out from the limb. Before Grey could shout a warning, his two companions were already in retreat and he was not far behind them, pausing only long enough to snatch up Pepe's machete, which might make him the victor in a hand-to-hand encounter.

They remained at a safe distance from the scene of action for some time before they were convinced that the snake was not pursuing. Then, proceeding with extreme caution, they returned to the tree. Under the limb were spatters of blood, but the giant snake was not to be found, nor had he left any trail when he retreated.

The men then turned their attention to the smaller snakes, beating the rocky ledges with long poles and branches until all the visible snakes had slipped off into the water. When the last snake had disappeared, they lifted the boat and carried it down the trail, around the first fall.

The succeeding falls were not so difficult, and in spite of the fear of watersnakes, the men voted in favor of floating the boat through and catching it from below as it shot over the falls. This was perilous work, for in addition to the snake hazard, there were many rocks covered with a slippery moss that made footing most uncertain. At one point, George shot out of the boat and into the water, and Grey, who was holding the tow-rope, could not manage the boat alone against the pull of the current. He was dragged over the slippery rocks and at last lodged against a stone, his eyes and mouth filled with the slimy water and his arms aching from the wrench of the current that had finally torn the tow-rope from his grasp. The boat shot over the ledge, heading straight toward Pepe, who was standing on a rock below, waiting to catch it after his comrades eased it over the edge.

With the boat out of control, however, it was approaching Pepe with such speed and force that Grey feared for the boatman's life. He tried to shout, but could not, and in the next instant the boat struck him head on. Pepe shot straight into the air, cleared the rock, and dropped into the water in a perfect dive, while the boat slipped over the mossy rock as easily as if it had been a wave, and lodged without injury on the bank below.

The men soon caught up with the boat, and when it was ascertained that their sturdy craft was still intact and that they themselves had escaped injury, they gave themselves up to laughter at their bedraggled appearance. Dripping and covered with slime, they sprawled on the bank roaring with merriment.

The reappearance of snakes sobered them, however, and they made haste to repack the boat and get it under way. Ahead were the rushing rapids of the main stream, and bright sunlight so hot that, by the time the half-mile course of rapids had been run, the travelers found that their clothing was completely dry and the cakes of mud could easily be brushed off.

Around the bend in the river they sighted a beautiful island, about two hundred yards long, with the river running in deep quiet channels on each side. The wide shoal and the shady cypresses were so inviting that Grey decided, then and there, that this was the spot he had been seeking as a more or less permanent camp. They needed a rest from their heavy labors.

A cursory exploration of the island revealed that there was an abundance of duck and other water fowl, an excellent campsite, a pile of driftwood that would make a quick campfire, and—best of all—not the sign of a snake or a tick.

The men were enthusiastic over their new home. They unpacked the boat completely, pitched camp in the shade of the leaning cypresses, and went their respective ways. Pepe began to prepare their supper. Grey lay in the shade of a tree, blissfully relaxed as he listened to the drowsy murmur of the current and the brooding notes of turtledoves. George took off on a one-man hunting expedition to bring in some ducks for the larder.

Grey awoke suddenly, surprised that he had fallen asleep so easily, and even more surprised to see George stripping off his clothing while both he and Pepe ferreted out ticks and popped them. They were inhabitants of the mainland, not the island, George made haste to explain. He had waded ashore in his hunt for ducks, and he had found, in addition to innumerable *garrapatas*, an abundance of ducks, wild turkeys, and evidence of the presence of tigers and wild pigs, the variety which Pepe called *javelin*. Even the fierceness of the ticks did not discourage George in the face of the hunting adventure that was to be found in the vicinity of the island. Grey promised him that they would all join in the hunt on the morrow, and promptly fell asleep again while George, with the boundless energy and curiosity of youth, tried his hand at fishing.

Their hunting adventures were due to begin before morning, however. Just at sunset, before they had finished their hearty repast of duck, canned fruit and vegetables, and hot cocoa, the ducks began to fly. There were all kinds: teal, canvas-backs, Muscovy ducks, and others that were unfamiliar to the Americans. Grey shot six in rapid succession, while George succeeded only in winging a few. Then, at Pepe's suggestion, they put out the campfire and sat quietly in the gathering darkness to watch and listen.

First came a long line of deer to drink at the water's edge. They sniffed the air, with an air more of curiosity than alarm, indicating that they scented the human invaders but did not know enough to fear them. Then Pepe's sharp eyes detected a herd of *javelin*, their green eyes gleaming eerily in the darkness. While they were splashing in the water, the jungle echoed with a weird, piercing wail that Grey recognized as the cry of a panther. The menacing sound was a signal for all activity to cease. Even the splashing of the *javelin* nearby was inaudible, as an ominous silence fell over the island. Then gradually movements resumed, and the listening hunters detected the click of deer hoofs, the yowl of a wildcat, the footsteps of wild pigs, and finally the hoarse, low growl that betrayed the presence of a jaguar and silenced all the lesser creatures of the jungle.

They did not see the jaguar that night, for although the voice came nearer and nearer to camp for a time, moonrise soon dispelled the darkness and made the island as bright as daylight, so discouraging nocturnal prowlers. But after breakfast the next morning they found in the soft sand, amidst hundreds of deer-tracks, the print of a jaguar's foot measuring larger across than Grey's hand. Even Pepe was amazed at the *"grande"* size of the print.

Grey determined to leave bait for the jaguar at the watering-place that night and lie in wait for him. Meanwhile, there was the mainland to explore.

It did not disappoint them. They had barely penetrated the first fringe of bamboo and palm when they came upon a herd of deer, half hidden by low bushes and tall grass. George handed his shotgun to Pepe, and quickly fired with his rifle. One deer went down, and the rest bounded away into the denser portion of the jungle.

After the first kill, more game appeared. There were more Muscovy ducks, a kind of pheasant that Pepe called "chicalocki," and wild turkeys. Grey was amazed to learn that the turkeys did not fly, but ran through the brush so swiftly that he missed them again and again, even at the comparatively short distance of fifty feet. It was not until he had shot several times that the great bronze turkeys finally took wing, in a roaring flight as beautiful as that of the familiar ruffed grouse of the Western plains. Against the sky they presented an easier target and Grey downed one.

In the midst of the excitement of the turkey hunt, Pepe shouted out: "*Javelin! Javelin!*" George began shooting into a cloud of dust from which emanated the sounds of trampling hoofs. As the cloud came nearer Pepe turned and fled for the river, carrying with him Grey's rifle. In an instant George made tracks to follow Pepe, and Grey, embarrassed as he was to flee from an unseen foe, could do nothing else since he had no rifle.

Breathless from the exertion of running, weighted down as he was by a shotgun and his prize turkey, he reached the boat where George and Pepe were already sitting ready to shove off. He was indignant at his comrades for running, but George assured him that he had shot one of the wild pigs and had surely wounded him, for he heard the animal squeal, and he knew that a wounded *javelin* is not to be tampered with. To this Pepe agreed, and in his terror even refused to go back for the deer carcass they had left lying in the trail.

The whole party was weary and short-tempered by the time they regained their island campsite. To make matters worse, they were covered with ticks. Building up the campfire, they hung their clothing near the blaze in order to singe as many of the insects as possible, meanwhile going to work with cigarette butts on the ones that clung to the flesh. Grey had accumulated his share:

broad bands of red *pinilius* around his ankles and huge patches of them on legs and arms. There were *garrapatas* too, a darker red than the *pinilius* and some of them as large as a copper penny.

Pepe was covered mostly with *pinilius*, and as usual, George with *garrapatas*. Grey ignored the smaller ticks on his own anatomy and went to work on the big fellows, plucking them off easily. Suddenly he felt a fiery stab of pain that seemed to penetrate his whole body and he emitted a tell-tale yell that made both of his comrades smile.

"That," George proclaimed, "was a *garrapata* bite."

Pepe covered his amusement quickly and came to the rescue, just in time to prevent Grey from pulling at the offending *garrapata*. Pepe explained that the creature had its head imbedded in the flesh and that it would be easy to remove the *garrapata's* body, leaving its head buried in the wound to cause a nasty infection.

Pepe had his own methods, tried and true, for dealing with such cases. He held the glowing tip of his cigarette near the tick; it wriggled and squirmed, and finally withdrew its head. Promptly Pete stabbed closer with the cigarette and the *garrapata* exploded. Of course, Grey was burned by the cigarette, but at least the tick was dead.

After scraping off the worst of the ticks, Pepe produced a bottle of *canyu*, a strong Mexican alcohol, with which they bathed their bodies. The sting of the fluid was worse than the bite of the insects, but it did not last long and the ticks did not return.

After a delectable feast of wild turkey and a midday siesta, Pepe summoned sufficient courage to return to the mainland and drag the deer's carcass down to the sand bar where the jaguar tracks had been seen. As dusk approached, the hunters concealed themselves behind rocks on the island, some fifty yards from the planted carcass.

Lying in wait, they refrained from conversation and even resisted the temptation to shoot at the wild fowl winging steadily above them. Darkness came, and the herd of deer returned to drink from the river. The moon rose and the deer moved quietly back into the jungle. A bank of clouds piled up in the sky and concealed the moon, leaving the jungle so dark that it was impossible to see the deer's carcass on the opposite shore. The men had separated and were watching from three different stations when out of the darkness of the mainland came a rustling sound, then a crunching as of a heavy body moving over the gravel at the water's edge. Grey could not perceive the slightest movement on the opposite bank, but suddenly George's rifle rang out, then Pepe's shotgun. Then for an instant Grey could see a gliding gray form on the sand bar. He threw several shots at it, but in the darkness could not be sure whether he had hit or missed his mark.

George and Pepe insisted that they had seen two tigers and that one of them had been hit—whether by George's shot or Pepe's, they were uncertain. But from the opposite shore they could hear no sound of a wounded animal, nor see evidence of dead game, so they returned to camp with the prospects of another night's vigil in their minds.

Early the next morning, Grey crossed the river and found that the carcass was gone. The tracks left in the sand were not those of the big jaguar, but of a panther who had dragged the carcass up the gravelly slope and then carried it off into the jungle without leaving a distinct trail.

Entering the jungle, Grey came upon a runway leading through a deep swale. In the runway were tiger tracks, and nearby under a bamboo clump, were piles of deer bones. This was the jaguar's feeding place. Thereupon Grey conceived the idea of baiting the runway with deer carcass and lying in wait there during the afternoon hours, all alone.

The first problem was to find the deer, but as it turned out, this was a simple matter, except for breaking through brush that was covered with ticks. Grey was spotted with them before he saw the herd of deer. He shot quickly and one of the deer fell, killed with the first shot. The *garrapatas* were biting by the time he had dragged the carcass back to the swale and placed it under the clump of bamboo, but he took time to carve off a haunch of venison and then hurried back to camp for the traditional tick treatment.

When the last tick had been destroyed, Grey soaked his hunting suit in kerosene to discourage further attacks and returned to the mainland to keep his lone vigil, without divulging the secret to Pepe and George, who would surely have insisted on accompanying him and might have frightened the game away.

The kerosene-drenched suit was suffocating and filled the air with a terrible stench. Moreover, it magnified the heat so that, by the time he reached the swale, Grey was forced to remove the coat. Then he settled back to wait.

Hours passed, and he forgot about the jaguar as he meditated upon the beauty of the jungle foliage. While he was dreamily counting the bamboo stalks a slight sound attracted his attention. Shifting his gaze, he was amazed to see the huge jaguar, poised with one paw on the deer carcass directly beneath the bamboo clump, not more than a hundred feet away.

The animal must have sensed the hunter's presence,

for he bared his fangs in an ominous growl. In that moment, Grey fired and a split second afterward saw the jaguar leap into the air with a terrifying roar. Grey shot a second time, and watched the animal fall to the ground and writhe about in the dust of the runway. He appeared to be in his death throes, but it was never wise to be too sure of a wounded animal. Grey put two more shot in him and reached for a fresh clip to re-load his automatic.

It was a matter of seconds to snap the loaded clip into place, but with the wounded jaguar lunging toward him, the seconds were an eternity. The animal was badly wounded, but he clung to his life and fought every inch of the way. There were not more than twenty-five feet between him and the hunter when Grey pumped a shell into the chamber and fired.

The shot only enraged the roaring animal. Roaring madly, coughing blood, he leaped once more toward his foe. Grey was seized with sudden panic, then adopted an air of forced calm, for it was apparent now that it must be either his life or the tiger's. He pumped three more shots into the plunging body. Then, with only one shot left in his rifle, he saw the animal leap up, only ten feet away, clawing the air, raging with fury and wheezing blood.

One more shot—and the jaguar leaped straight at the hunter, coughing blood all over him. Then he fell down, down, into the hollow.

Grey could no longer see him, but as he loaded fresh clips he could hear the jaguar threshing around in the thick foliage below. Then the movement stopped and Grey, assuming he was dead, stepped closer. But the swaying of the brush gave proof that the jaguar was still alive, and slinking back into the jungle.

Grimly, the hunter looked down at his blood-spattered clothing and realized that this was the closest escape he had known in all his hunting days. He was shaken and ill. Then courage and determination returned; he would not let that wounded jaguar get away from him, after the long battle he had put up. At least, he must put the beast out of his agony.

Re-loading the automatic, he followed the bloody trail of the jaguar into the jungle. He could hear it ahead of him, dragging its heavy body through the dense brush, and he took the precaution of moving only when the jaguar moved, stopping to listen at every few steps, lest the wounded animal lie in wait for him. In his eagerness, he had left his coat behind, so his shirt was soon torn from his shoulders and his body covered with ticks. Still he kept on.

Two things forced him to give up the chase. One was the realization that darkness was creeping up on the jungle, and that in another hour it would be impossible to find his way back to the river. The other was the fierce stabbing pains that struck him as the giant *garrapatas* sank their heads into the tender flesh across his shoulders and upper arms. Without taking time to retrieve his coat, he made all possible haste to the river and thence back to camp, a sorry sight to confront his astonished companions.

He removed his tattered clothing and saw by the firelight the myriad spots all over his body. Pepe knew exactly what to do. First he sloshed a bucket of cold water all over Grey's body. Then he asked him to point out the ticks that were biting hardest, and he and George went to work with lighted cigarettes. Between them, they burned up five cigarettes before the biting had stopped, and still there were ticks clinging for dear life.

The last phase of the treatment was a quick bath in the fiery *canyu,* then into clean pajamas and bed, reclining as he told his comrades the tale of the day's adventure.

With the potent liquid burning his skin, it was a long time before Grey fell asleep. When he did, his exhaustion was so great that he did not awaken until the sun was high the next morning—ten hours later. He was surprised to find no after-effects except a great laziness and the desire for peace and quiet. To achieve this desired state, he suggested that George have Pepe row him along the shaded bank of the mainland and see what game they might scare up. This idea was met with enthusiasm, even by George who had not been feeling well for a couple of days, and the two shoved off in the boat, leaving Grey to lapse into slumber once more.

He was awakened by the sound of a rifle shot. Upstream about two hundred yards away he saw the boat drifting along, but only Pepe was in it. George was nowhere to be seen, but again his rifle cracked and Grey became aware from the whine of the bullet that whatever George was shooting at, he was in the line of fire. Hastily he took refuge behind the thickest of the cypresses, meanwhile shouting out a warning to George to mind where he was shooting.

Either George did not hear or was too excited to pay attention, for the shots were repeated. Drifting downstream toward the island, Pepe appeared tremendously excited over the scene on the mainland. When he had drifted near enough to be within shouting distance, Grey again called out to learn the cause of the furor. Pepe said he did not know what George was shooting at, but it was "something big."

Just then George cried: "Look out on the island! I'll be shooting that way!"

94

Grey scarcely had time to duck behind his favorite tree when the bullets began flying again, uncomfortably close. Without peeping out to look, he yelled at George, "What are you aiming at?"

It was Pepe who answered, in shrill tones. *"Tigre! Tigre!"*

Daring to venture forth, Grey looked out at the mainland in time to see the flashing yellow body crash through the brush toward the water. Then George appeared back of the brush, shouting at Pepe, "Where is he? Where is he?"

Despite Grey's shouted warnings to George to stay out of the brush, the excited boy dived in, heading in the direction Pepe was pointing. Grey saw a movement of the yellow body in the brush in front of George; he took quick aim with his rifle and fired. He knew from the blood-curdling cry and the threshing of the foliage that he had hit his mark. George had halted and was taking aim when the jaguar tore from the brush and leaped into the river.

Grey could see the yellow head rising above water, but he dared not shoot for the jaguar was in the direct line with the boat. He shouted at Pepe to shoot, but Pepe merely waved the shotgun frantically in the air, too excited to take aim. But the jaguar was swimming toward the boat, thus providing new incentive for Pepe to practice his marksmanship. Encouraged by Grey's shouted instructions from the island, Pepe grasped the double-barreled shotgun in more or less correct position and pulled both triggers at once. Both shots went wild, but the kick of the gun sent Pepe sprawling backward and into the water.

He was still in a direct line with the jaguar, making it impossible for Grey to shoot. George meanwhile was standing helplessly on the bank, his rifle jammed at the crucial moment.

Pepe might have swum around indefinitely except for the swirls in the water that reminded him of the alligator they had frequently seen thereabouts. Between alligator and jaguar, he chose the jaguar and pulled himself up to the boat.

"Hit him with an oar!" Grey howled. "Keep him in the water! Don't let him in the boat!"

But Pepe heard not a word. With the jaguar coming closer, he swung the boat toward shore, just close enough to permit him to grasp the overhanging limb of a tree and go scrambling to safety just as the jaguar struck the boat. For an instant the low-hanging boughs made a screen that obscured Pepe, the boat, and the animal, so Grey was still helpless to do anything. Then he heard George's rifle crack again and again, followed each time with the sound of bullets spatting against wood, so even though Grey could not see the scene on the opposite shore he knew that George was not hitting the jaguar and could very probably be hitting the boat.

"Watch out!" he yelled. "You'll sink the boat!"

But George kept on shooting.

Then the boat swung free of the branches, drifted downstream a short distance, and into the bank. Pepe climbed down from his tree and caught the boat, and while he was thus engaged George disappeared again into the brush.

Grey called to Pepe to come and get him, and together they rowed back to the mainland to search for George and his jaguar. They found George, white and shaking with excitement, but they lost the trail of the jaguar. George was reluctant to give up, but was finally persuaded to return to camp when he learned that the boat, filled with bullet-holes from his rifle, was half filled with water already.

Grey spent the evening patching up the boat with whittled pegs while George prowled restlessly about, mourning over the jaguar that got away. He was sure that it was the biggest jaguar in the jungle, but Grey had to deny that, for he knew it did not approach the size of the jaguar that had lunged at him on the jungle trail the preceding day

During the night Grey was awakened by the rattling of tin pans. He knew instantly that some animal must have invaded their camp, and with gun in hand he ran from the tent, followed by George. Pepe was already standing outside the tent, staring at the churning water at the river's edge. Grey knew at once what had happened. The alligator they had seen from time to time had paid their camp a visit. Pepe had awakened to see it only ten feet from their open tent. Like all the natives, Pepe had a horror of alligators and reiterated frantically that they were man-eaters. He insisted on keeping watch the rest of the night, and since the frightened man would probably not have slept anyway, Grey made no objection. The marauder did not return, however, and the rest of the night was passed quietly.

Morning came, and with it news that killed all the joys of the hunting expedition. George was ill. Grey was of the opinion that the boy had been eating too much fresh meat or that he had been careless about drinking river water without boiling it, but Pepe disagreed with the diagnosis. According to him, all the symptoms—aching bones, abdominal cramps, upset stomach, coated tongue, and violent headache—pointed to tropic fever. George sadly nodded corroboration. He knew what it was; he had had it before.

No more hunting was done on the island. George was a very sick boy and required constant attention. Grey did the best he could with the limited medicine supply he had brought, and as he ministered to the young man he turned over in his mind the possible courses of action.

They must get George back to civilization as quickly as possible. To go back upstream over the route they had come down would be impossible, with a sick man to carry and care for. Going downstream, according to their original plan, might prove just as bad, but it could not be worse. So he determined to continue onward, trusting to luck to see them through.

As soon as George was able to walk, they broke camp and left the island. Gloomily Grey recalled the contrasting high spirits with which they had first landed on the island and selected their "home." He knew that some day he would want to come back to Cypress Island, but realistically he turned his attention to the problem at hand.

The trip downstream was rendered more hazardous by the increasing number of alligators, in addition to swift rapids and jutting rocks in the channel. In guiding the boat over the shallower falls, Grey sometimes had to get out and wade in waters where he knew alligators were numerous, but necessity gave him the courage he required. Pepe, too, became more courageous and dared to step into the water to help with the boat. At one of the steeper drops, he jumped over the ledge to catch the boat from below, as Grey guided it over. Grey heard the Mexican emit a horrible scream and, looking down, saw that Pepe had stepped upon an alligator. The lashing tail hurled Pepe into the stream, and while Pepe swam desperately for the rocks, Grey emptied his gun at the alligator and watched it vanish in the pool.

When they pitched camp at the end of the first day, Grey calculated they had traveled a good forty miles, but it had been forty miles of nightmare to him. He determined to beat that record on the second day, and with that goal in mind, roused his companions before dawn in order to make an early start.

If the first day was a nightmare, the second was worse. Everything went wrong. They encountered the worst falls they had found throughout the entire expedition, and a series of deep, narrow rapids. At one point they were caught in a whirlpool and, unable to row out of it, Pepe lassoed a stump and pulled them out. About midday came the worst mishap of all.

Grey was guiding the boat through a narrow rapid while his comrades walked around and waited below. The boat swung dangerously near a huge rock that was half-submerged in the channel and try as he might Grey could not avert the catastrophe. The boat struck—but instead of splintering, it glanced off the rock with nothing but a dull thud. Before Grey could recover from this surprise, there was a great churning of the water, the boat heaved suddenly upward, then settled back in the water with a splash that splintered the gunwale. As the boat raised up, Grey saw the cause of the commotion. Underneath was an alligator, eight feet long and every inch of him furious. He had obviously been sleeping on the rock when the boat came too near and disturbed his slumbers.

Seeing him at close quarters, Grey made a startling and unpleasant discovery. The "alligators" they had been dodging were not alligators at all—they were crocodiles. His comrades were not interested in the fine distinction. They were perturbed at the condition of the boat, which was rapidly filling with water. They had to carry the boat ashore, unload it, and repair the split gunwale, a task that could not be hurried.

Nervous over the accident that had caused this unforeseen delay, Grey pushed onward. The river became smoother for a time, but crocodiles were more numerous than ever. Then along the river bank they sighted trails which, according to Pepe, were cattle trails. This was a promising sign, for it was well known that wild cattle grazed all along the Panuco River. Soon a herd of them appeared at the water's edge to give added hope that the travelers were not too far from the point where the Santa Rosa flowed into the Panuco.

The jungle was no longer dense and green; vegetation was sparser and of a duller hue. Herds of cattle appeared at every turn in the river. Frequently there were places where the cattle had mired down in the soft mud and were slowly dying of starvation, while buzzards circled around ready to close in. Putrefied carcasses were to be seen all along the river, and occasionally there was the horrible sight of cattle gone crazy from ticks in their ears. Grey's humane instincts rebelled against these sights and he wanted desperately to put the creatures out of their misery, but Pepe warned him that Mexican law forbade the killing of cattle.

With these almost certain signs of approaching civilization, George rallied and began to take potshots at crocodiles. He and Grey shared the ambition to take home a crocodile hide, and so they spent some time rowing around hunting for easy targets. They hit many, but learned to their chagrin that crocodiles cling to life even more tenaciously than jaguars. Filled with bullet-holes, they would still thrash about in the water and then disappear.

This increased the hunters' determination to bag one.

They became so intent upon the kill that they began shooting at every log they saw, for they had observed that enormous logs and bits of driftwood had a way of coming to life and swimming away before their eyes. Grey took a rather careless shot at an unusually large log and found to his surprise that he had hit a crocodile and wounded it seriously. He and George jumped from the boat and stood on the bank, firing shot after shot at the reptile until their ammunition was exhausted. By all rights, their target should have been dead, but still its thick tail flailed the water and it appeared that one more wounded victim was going to make his get-away into the deeper waters of the stream.

Grey had a sudden inspiration. Shouting to Pepe in the boat, he instructed: "Get your rope! Lasso him!"

Quick as a wink, Pepe had his rope around one of the crocodile's heavy flippers. Grey and George leaped back into the boat to lend a hand, as the struggling reptile pulled the rope taut. It was a game of tug-of-war in which both sides were winning: the crocodile was making off down river, and his adversaries were being towed along behind.

George was hilarious. "All aboard for Panuco!" he cried, as the boat gathered speed.

"You won't need to row any more, Pepe," Grey exulted. "We have a water horse now."

With the rope tied securely around the bowsprit, the boat was moving as fast as the crocodile could swim. Pepe, being chief oarsman, should have been pleased, but there was a look of foreboding on his face. He did not trust crocodiles.

His mistrust was soon justified. Out in midstream, where the channel was deep, the bow suddenly dipped into the water and the stern shot up in the air at a forty-five-degree angle. The crocodile was diving to the bottom and dragging the boat with him.

"Cut the rope!" Grey shouted wildly, but Pepe could not even find his machete at the moment. Grey grasped his own knife, leaped over Pepe, and cut the rope just as the water began rushing into the bow. The boat righted itself immediately, but there were six inches of water in the bottom—so once more Grey called a halt to attend to boat repairs.

Sundown that evening found them several miles farther downstream and pitching camp on a convenient sand bar. They were fortunate in finding such a campsite, free from ticks and from cattle tracks, but Grey's mind was filled with a vague unrest, a sense of impending disaster. He was obsessed with the necessity to keep pushing along downriver with all possible speed, yet there seemed no good reason for the feeling, for George was faring better and Pepe, though tired and unusually quiet, was holding up very well.

The next day he helped Pepe with the rowing, not only to give the *mozo* a chance to rest but to give himself something to do. With hard rowing, they managed to cover thirty miles by four o'clock, and at sundown they were again fortunate enough to find a favorable campsite on a rocky promontory where firewood was abundant and a clear spring provided the first decent drinking water they had had for many a day.

While Grey pitched camp, Pepe went into the forest for firewood and George, hearing Pepe shout some time later, followed after to see if there was any game worth shooting at. Soon Grey heard their mingled shouts and, loading his rifle, he went running into the woods in search of his companions.

As he drew nearer he could make out their voices.

"*Javelin!*" Pepe was shouting. "*Santa Maria!*" At the same time George was calling out, "Wild pigs! Wild pigs! We're treed! Run for your life!"

Grey could not help recalling their first encounter with wild pigs back at Cypress Island, when his comrades had made him run from the unseen herd. The thought still rankled and he reacted stubbornly. "I'll be darned if I'll run!" he replied.

Despite the repeated warnings and the pleading tones of Pepe and George, he came closer until he could see the two men perched in their respective strongholds high above the ground. But still he could see no wild pigs.

He began to suspect a hoax, for although George insisted that the herd was directly beneath them under the trees, Grey could neither see nor hear them.

"I'll scare them away," he offered, and promptly fired several shots into the brush beneath the trees.

Any doubts he had had as to the honesty of his companions were soon dispelled. There was a roaring and squealing, a tramping of hoofs, and a cloud of dust. Then the bushes parted in a hundred places, and everywhere he looked Grey could see a darting gray animal. He emptied his automatic at them, but even though every shot went home, it scarcely made a dent in the horde. For every *javelin* that went down, six bobbed up to take its place. There was nothing to do but to run.

Down the slope he ran, stumbling, falling, rolling over and over, with the vicious pigs gaining ground all the while. At last he saw a low branch, leaped up and swung himself up into the tree, from which he could look down at the mean little brutes with their sharp noses and gleaming tusks. From the safety of his perch, he shot down at them, killing a pig with each shot, but he soon reflected upon the futility of this, for he had fifty shots at most and there were hundreds of pigs milling about below.

In answer to the shouts of George and Pepe, Grey assured them that he was all right—treed just as they were. George, shouting back, informed him that all the pigs had followed after him, leaving the coast clear for them to climb down and retreat to camp for their guns. "Don't risk it," Grey replied—and in that instant he saw that the frail branch that upheld him was cracking away from the tree trunk and could not support his weight much longer. No other refuge was in sight. He knew what would happen if he dropped down in the midst of those trampling hoofs.

In desperation he called out to his companions, describing his predicament in a few words. He knew that the *javelin* would have to be frightened away if his own life was to be saved, but how to do it was another question.

Then Pepe's shrill yell assailed his ears, and simultaneously the flicker of a flame appeared up the slope in the direction from which he had fled. Grey's first thought was that Pepe had set the brush on fire, but to his amazement he saw the *mozo* advancing upon the herd of pigs, shouting and brandishing a flaming torch.

The ruse was successful. It was a matter of moments for the whole herd to go thundering away into the woods. As Grey started to lower himself from the branch, it broke and he fell to the ground at Pepe's feet.

He scarcely had time to express his gratitude to the plucky Pepe before discovering that the jungle behind them was blazing, having caught fire from Pepe's torch. Grey had a peculiar horror of forest fires, but Pepe merely shrugged his shoulders and commented that it would harm nothing but ticks, while George observed that there would be plenty of roast pig by morning.

The fire did not gain great headway and there was no danger from it on the rocky ledge where their camp was pitched. But the camp was nonetheless an unfortunate location, as it turned out, for it was the object of an attack by monstrous black mosquitoes. Pepe seemed to fear them as much as he did alligators or *tigres*, and all his heroic efforts to smoke them out were to no avail. They swarmed all over the camp. Sleep that night was impossible. The only thing the men could do in self-defense was to sit within the smoke of the campfire.

Morning found them more weary than they had been the night before. Pepe was listless and had no appetite, and George had definitely taken a turn for the worse. Grey was convinced that this was the answer to his strange premonitions of the past two days, and he made all haste to break camp and start down river. He made a bed for George in the bottom of the boat and then took turns at the oars to give Pepe a chance to rest.

They made good time, and shortly after noon they spied a thatched hut on the bank, with naked little Indians peering out. There were more huts later on, and after a couple of hours of rowing, they reached a broad river, twice as wide as the Santa Rosa and with a swifter current. Grey was convinced that they had at last reached the Panuco, especially after glimpsing tarpon in the waters.

High on a bluff overlooking the river was a large hut, and to this hut they made their way after beaching the boat on a sand bar. The inhabitants were both curious and hospitable. They offered the travelers chicken soup and hot milk, and gave them vague information as to their location. It was, they said, two days and two nights by canoe to the village of Panuco.

George and Pepe wanted to spend the night there, but Grey was eager to move on. At nightfall he almost regretted the decision, for there was no campsite to be found. He met the situation by ordering the other two to make their beds in the boat while he rowed.

All night long he rowed in darkness, while his comrades slept. He was aware of the dangers around him, but he kept his ear tuned for the slightest change in the sound of the current and gained confidence as the miles flowed by without mishap. At daybreak he was still rowing, though his back was stiff and his arms ached.

He found a good place to stop for breakfast and wakened his companions, but George could not move from the boat. Pepe and Grey ate hastily, in gloomy silence, then shoved off again. This time Pepe took the oars while Grey slept, exhausted from the long night's toil.

Occasionally they passed crude canoes paddled by natives, who gave them varied and unreliable reports on the distance to Panuco. Some said two days' journey, some said "Far, far away," and others said it was "just around the next bend." In view of the contradictory information, Grey was reluctant to camp another night, for George was not improved. They stopped briefly for supper, then rowed on, Grey and Pepe taking turns at rowing and sleeping. Some time during the night, while Pepe was at the oars, the boat struck a sandbar, and in their utter weariness they decided to let it rest there while they slept until morning.

There was another day of hard rowing, with no sign of a village in sight and nothing to break the monotony except occasional canoes full of natives, none of whom seemed to know the exact distance to Panuco. That night, too tired to row, they slept on a sandbar without even bothering to pitch a tent.

At noon of the next day, aching in every muscle, suffering from exposure to the sun for days, parched with thirst, they spotted a village. This, they learned, was Panuco. They had come to the end of the journey.

It was but a brief ride by cart to the railroad station at Tamos, and from Tamos only a matter of a few hours to Tampico, where medical care could be secured for George Allen and peaceful rest awaited Pepe and Grey. A native was engaged to row the boat, with the heavier equipment, down the river to Tampico.

They had covered more than two hundred miles of river in less than two weeks, the majority of it unknown to man, and the worst part of it under the greatest anxiety for the welfare of their sick passenger. Every day of the journey had held more adventure than the average man meets in the course of a lifetime. Yet much as he looked forward to the well-deserved rest in Tampico, Grey felt a certain wistfulness as he turned his back on the lonely jungle river.

The Fisherman

Long after the Santa Rosa expedition had taken its place in Zane Grey's treasury of memories, he re-worked his notes on the day-by-day happenings of the memorable trip and published them under the title, "Down an Unknown Jungle River" in a non-fiction volume titled *Tales of Southern Rivers*. The same notes also provided the background for *Ken Ward in the Jungle*, another novel in the increasingly popular series of Ken Ward books for boys. In this fictionalized version of the expedition, Ken Ward was once more Zane Grey in disguise; George Allen became George Alling, and Pepe was the same faithful *mozo* who had lost his reputation through drunkenness and regained his self-respect through the trust of his American employer. The major change in the story for fiction purposes was the addition of a fourth member to the party: Hal Ward, younger brother of Ken, joined the expedition to collect botanical specimens in the jungles.

Besides providing Grey with material for his writing, these adventures in Mexico satisfied his longing to explore strange new places and whetted his appetite for

He was as proud of catching a five-pound steelhead
as a five-hundred-pound tuna.

He became as fine a shot as any of his frontiersmen ancestors, but his interest was in conserving wild life rather than exterminating it.

fishing. He had always been interested in fishing, from the time of his boyhood when he fished in the Muskingum River near Zanesville and in the Delaware at Lackawaxen. Later he developed a particular interest in big-game fishing, a sport that had been denied him throughout his years of stringent economy. But now, with a steady income from his books, articles, and magazine serials, he could afford to make one more dream come true. The tarpon fishing at Tampico was only the beginning of his fishing adventures.

He set out to explore the mysteries of the open sea as eagerly as he had first set out to explore the great plains of the West. It was true, as he himself confessed, that he could never do anything by half-measures. When he made up his mind to do a thing, he worked at it wholeheartedly and with a singleness of purpose that insured success in each new venture. So, when he decided to try his hand at deep-sea fishing, he was determined that this was to be no amateurish attempt. He was not content to be just another fisherman; he wanted to be a good fisherman.

With this aim in mind, he spent months corresponding with professional fishermen and topnotch anglers on the fine points of technique, bait, and equipment. He made an exhaustive study of all the technical works he could find on the subject, building up an immense collection of books on angling, of which he found those by English authors most helpful. It was said that he had more fishing books than fishing rods, though he had so many of the latter that he frequently lost count. He haunted sporting goods shops examining different kinds of tackle and asking questions about their relative merits. Then he went out to learn more in the school of experience and to record his findings in volumes of non-fiction narrative that provided accurate and detailed information for the benefit of the novice.

He fished in the Gulf of Mexico and in the Caribbean, off the Canadian Pacific coast and the shores of Nova Scotia. He spent summers at picturesque Avalon, fishing the waters around Catalina Island for barracuda, white sea-bass, tuna, and broadbill swordfish. Whenever possible, he wintered at Long Key, Florida, a lonely white coral reef where he loved to roam along the beach and to go fishing for tarpon, sharks, and marlin. One year he was fishing with his friend Bob Davis, then editor of *Munsey's Magazine*, off the New Jersey coast when the *Lusitania* swept by them down the channel. The passengers leaned over the rail to wave and shout, for they could see that Grey was engaged in battle with a fish that had bent his rod double. Grey lost the fish, and the gigantic ocean liner disappeared from the horizon, headed for its doom.

During a fishing jaunt to Long Key one winter, the houseboat of John Wanamaker was pointed out to Grey. As a student at the University of Pennsylvania he had often wandered through the famous Wanamaker Store, but he had never dreamed of meeting its owner. Even when he found that they were, figuratively speaking, rubbing elbows at the fishing resort, he still entertained no thought of meeting the wealthy Philadelphian.

But one day a message came to Zane Grey, requesting him to call upon Mr. Wanamaker. He was nearly overcome with curiosity as well as shyness, for even his years of success had not given him the self-confidence to meet people easily.

His curiosity was somewhat assuaged when he entered the cabin of the luxurious houseboat and saw on the desk a copy of his own *Tales of Fishes*. There was the explanation. Mr. Wanamaker, who was a fishing enthusiast himself, probably wanted to compare notes on technique or take issue with him on some point mentioned in the book.

The author was prepared to defend his work, or to argue, but he was not prepared for the brief interview that followed when John Wanamaker, ageing and white-haired, entered the room and greeted him. The older man made no reference to the book that lay on the desk, but laying a friendly hand on his guest's shoulder, said:

"Zane Grey, you are distinctively and genuinely American. I am happy to see that you have borrowed none of the decadence of foreign writers. I have given away thousands of your books and I have sold hundreds of thousands in my store. The good you are doing is incalculable, Zane Grey. *Never lay down your pen!*"

The unexpected words of Mr. Wanamaker left him half-stunned, half-embarrassed, and he found himself incapable of making an appropriate reply, for Zane Grey, at home with the written word, lost all his courage and presence of mind in a verbal encounter. He was essentially a man of action, and he was consequently far more at ease in a battle with a jaguar or a man-eating shark than in a struggle to express himself in spoken words. Out in the open, whether engaged in landing a giant game fish or talking to fellow hunters around the camp-fire, he lost his self-consciousness, forgetting himself in his absorption with the adventure of the moment. But in a formal atmosphere, in a crowd, or even in a personal interview when attention was focused upon Zane Grey as a personality, he became as diffident and retiring as he had been as an awkward freshman in college.

He was humbly grateful for the tributes paid him by his many readers, but warming as these experiences were to remember, they were uncomfortable to face. It was a long time before he even mentioned his meeting with Wanamaker and his own stumbling response to the great man's words. Returning to his own craft, he said not a word about it, even to his brother R.C., who happened to be with him on this excursion.

They were bound this winter for a cruise of the Gulf Stream which abounded in sailfish, marlin, mola-mola, and orca. Concentrating on the expedition, Zane Grey made a study of the whale-killing orca, known to be dangerous to man and fish alike, and known even to have charged upon fishing boats occasionally. All seafaring men hated them and even veteran whale-hunters feared them. So many were the tales of this menace that the orca had become a sea legend, almost mythical to the inexperienced.

There was nothing mythical about their behavior, however. They were vicious and fearful things, as indicated in Zane Grey's notes on observations made during the excursion. "Orca," he wrote, "kill for the sake of killing. No doubt the Creator created them, the same as sharks, to preserve a balance in the species of the Seven Seas—to teach all the larger fish and dolphin, seals, porpoises, that the price of life was eternal vigilance. But when you know that the mackerel and menhaden are gone, to make oil, and the albacore are gone, and the white sea bass are wasted for fertilizer, and that the tuna are disappearing, and that one fleet of purse-net boats caught seven million pounds of barracuda last October—without lowering the price of fish one cent per pound —and that no matter how much you would like to kill the Austrians and Japs who are robbing our seas to make a few men rich, you cannot do it,—under these circumstances it does not seem outrageous to put a grim ban on orca. At any rate, some of the scientific experts on ocean fish claim the orca should be killed."

Prevented from killing the odious orca, Zane Grey and his brother determined to photograph the sea-killer in action. One day they came upon a school of orca, glistening black in the green water, huge spear-like fins protruding ten feet above the water's level. These vanished, then reappeared, sometimes coming close enough to the launch to enable the excited spectators to discern their peculiar black-and-white markings, but usually keeping at a tantalizing distance.

Grey gave the order and the chase began, the boat's captain pursuing the fleeting school at top speed. After an hour of maneuvering, they came close enough to the school to ascertain that there were six orca in all, one of which was much larger than his fellows, almost whale-like in appearance. "We're going to photograph that big fellow," Grey promised his brother. Never in all their fishing experiences had they been any more excited.

They snapped pictures rashly, long before they were within range. Then, when they were near enough to make out the vicious features of the giant orca with the distinguishing white mark at the side of its jaw, they found that the killer was too quick, too elusive to permit more than a quick glimpse, much less a photograph of any value.

Doggedly they followed the school, circling around it, turning to meet it head-on, never losing sight of it. The task they had set for themselves required more time and patience than to hook a game fish, and possibly an equal amount of skill. At last their efforts were rewarded. Approaching within a hundred feet of the school, they saw the huge fins cleave the water as two of the smaller orca curved upward over the crest of a wave. An instant later, the giant orca appeared, breaking through the water's surface. In a tense moment R.C. and Zane Grey held their cameras poised, and a moment later they saw the gigantic form lunge clear of the water, describing a perfect arc in the air. Two shutters clicked simultaneously, and when the films were developed later, the two fishermen were as proud of their pictures as they would have been of the fish itself, captured alive.

"If I fished only to capture fish," the author wrote later, "my fishing trips would have ended long ago." This remark was not made in reference to the orca, but to an incident that occurred later that winter, during the same expedition, when he and R.C. had followed the inland rivers of Florida into the Everglades, fishing and exploring these little-known waters. One evening, after a discouraging day of unsuccessful casting, Grey proved that he was indeed a "hard-luck" fisherman when he hooked a fish and then lost it, despite all his own skill and R.C.'s excited coaching from the sidelines. But the loss of the fish meant nothing to him compared to the memory he carried with him of the leaping fish outlined against a background of "a sunlit, cloud-mirroring green-and-gold bordered cove." To his artistic nature, the beauty of the scene was infinitely more satisfying than the glory of the catch.

In an introspective mood he discovered that fishing meant more to him than the excitement of a record catch or the privilege of feasting his eyes on beautiful scenery. These expeditions afforded him an opportunity to see new places, to learn new things. And through the medium of his works, he wanted to pass along to the stay-at-homes the gleanings of information from his adventures. Recalling the words of John Wanamaker, and the letters he had received from readers in all walks of life, he was reminded that he owed something to his faithful readers, and that entertainment alone was not enough. In the same spirit of sharing that had given him pleasure to provide baseball thrills for spectators who, because of physical handicaps or lack of leisure time, had never been able to play the game, he now was conscious of wanting his readers to feel the thrill of adventure as he felt it, to see each scene and to sense the atmosphere as vividly as if they were accompanying him on each expedition. But thrills and excitement were only a part of the adventure. They must learn new things as he learned. Like Robert Louis Stevenson, whom he admired so greatly, he believed that the proper function of a writer is to "inform while entertaining."

So, wherever he went, he kept his eyes and ears open for all kinds of information—geographical, historical, nature lore, folk lore, and legend. While maintaining his position as foremost author of Western romances, he was making a reputation for himself in quite a different field. He was winning world renown as a sportsman and writer. People were inclined to look upon him as a combined explorer and globe-trotting correspondent, engaging in his favorite sports as he traveled, but including in his narratives all phases of the life he lived and saw.

When he wrote of fishing in the Gulf Stream, he did not confine himself to tales of fishes, but described the setting in such a way that the Gulf Stream became to his readers a real geographical phenomenon rather than a vague abstraction half-remembered from a fifth-grade geography text. Through Zane Grey's eyes, they saw the great stream as a river within the Gulf—a river fifty miles wide, bordered by sea rather than by land, distinct in itself because of its rapid motion and its blue color, in contrast to the ocean's green. They learned the direction of its current, the appearance of its trade-wind clouds, and the variety of its marine life. He pictured for them the schools of flying-fish, and the Portuguese man-of-war with its parasitic "butterfly fish" attached. He told them what kind of bait to use for different fish and how to cut it; what kind of gear was best and why.

When he wrote of his fishing trip through the rivers and lagoons of the Everglades, he imparted not only the feeling of discouragement over "the fish that got away," but clear-cut impressions of the flora and fauna as well as the aquatic life, and in addition a knowledge of the Seminole Indians, their history, their culture, and their way of life in the swamplands. The reader is given food for thought in Grey's sober observation that "The old story of white aggression to possess valuable lands belonging to the Indians is as true in relation to the Seminoles as it ever was in the West."

Such remarks made it clear that Zane Grey regarded his fellow man with something more than passive curiosity. He had a profound interest in all the peoples of the earth; his humane sympathies knew no bounds of nationality, race, or culture. The problems of the Seminole Indian or the Mexican boatman were as real to him as the problems of an Arizona rancher. He believed that in all men there is a rough, primitive nature that remains as a carry-over from the age he called "the savage past," and that this primitive nature occasionally breaks through the veneer of civilization. But in the course of evolution, Nature, in order to counterbalance the primal instinct, provided man with conscience. This was the sublime touch, the divine spark that guided man from his lowest depths of savagery to heights of nobility when occasion demanded. He believed in the basic decency of people. His faith in their ability to progress was indicative of his belief in the power of conscience over primitive inheritance.

He had read widely of the races and peoples inhabiting the remote corners of the earth, but he was not content to read about them. He had to meet them and talk with them. Second-hand views were unsatisfactory; he had to see for himself.

Some day, he vowed, he would travel to those faraway lands. He would sail the Seven Seas in his own white-sailed ship. "There was a Lorelei calling, . . . a siren bell ringing from the abysmal deep."

Across Death Valley

"To awake from pleasant dreams," wrote Grey, with wistful resignation, "that is the lot of man."

He bore his lot with good grace, but he was restless to answer the Lorelei voice. The war years, however, prevented extensive travel outside the United States so he was forced to spend his wanderlust urge in his own country and its coastal waters. Summers he spent at Avalon, living in his Indian adobe home, writing, and fishing off Catalina Island. His brother, R.C., who often aided him in his business affairs, joined him for the fishing season. It was a record one in 1917, with an abundance of barracuda, sea-bass, yellowtail, broadbill swordfish, tuna, and marlin.

The following year, though not an outstanding one at Avalon, was quite satisfying and provided the author with the variety he needed and the opportunity to indulge in what was rapidly becoming his favorite hobby. In August he turned from deep-sea fishing and went with R.C. and a friend, "Lone Angler" Wiborn, to Vancouver Island, stopping off in Washington State for a couple of weeks to fish for the elusive steelheads of Deer River.

The winter months found him fishing off the coast of Florida, spending the major part of his time on the lonely coral island of Long Key where he loved to bask in the warm sunlight of the beach, gather seashells, and day-dream. It was a relaxing atmosphere; its quiet peaceful-ness helped him to collect his thoughts and invariably inspired him to write.

Being a very serious man, as well as a red-blooded American, he was profoundly affected by the World War. He was, by that time, beyond service age, and the only weapon he could use was his pen, but he used that more steadily and conscientiously than ever before, with the realization that his books provided inspiration and escape for homesick boys in army camps and for the troops in the trenches overseas, where Zane Grey "West-erns" were unanimously voted favorite reading. His mild, peace-loving nature rebelled against the forces that had thrown the world into a state of chaos, destroying the lives of thousands of sturdy American boys, disrupt-ing the careers and homes of thousands more. He was more keenly aware of the tragic loss of the cream of American youth because he had such high hopes for his own two sons—Romer, who was in his ninth year, and the little boy Loren, barely a year old when the United States cast her lot with the Allies. Thinking of the fu-ture of his boys, he was overcome with sympathy for parents who raised their sons to manhood, only to send them into battle to be killed or, what was often much worse, crippled in body or in spirit. He deplored the needless wreckage of humanity and bore a bitter, resent-ful hatred for the German nation.

All his anti-German sentiment was poured out in his major wartime novel, *The Desert of Wheat*, with its setting in the fertile wheat fields of the Columbia River

Basin, between the magnificent Cascade Mountains on the west and the picturesque Coeur d'Alene country on the east.

Kurt Dorn, the youthful hero of the novel, was torn between two loyalties: that of a patriotic American to his country in time of war, and that of a son whose German-born father, though a naturalized American, clings to the old ties of his fatherland and betrays his adopted country. Knowing that his work on the wheat ranch was vitally necessary to provide the staff of life for fighting men, Kurt still felt under obligation to enlist in order to prove his own patriotism and to atone, indirectly, for the pro-German activities of his father. Before he could enlist, however, he was caught in the web of international intrigue, battling against a traitorous foreign element that was attempting, with the aid of Kurt's father, to gain a foothold in this vast wheat-producing region for the purpose of sabotaging the war production program. Despite the reputation Kurt gained by organizing vigilante committees of patriotic ranchers in the Valley to check the invasion of the saboteurs, he carried out his promise to himself to leave the ranch in good hands and enlist for overseas service. After a brief but horrible experience in the front lines, he was sent home with shell-shock that threatened to destroy his mind and physical wounds that threatened to destroy his body. The serenity of the golden desert of wheat and the unfaltering devotion of the woman he loved accomplished the miracle, and Kurt Dorn, with his mind free from the turmoil and phantom fears that had beset him, settled down on his beloved ranch.

The mental struggle of Kurt Dorn was probably quite similar to the struggle being waged in the mind of the author himself, who had learned to hate so intensely, and yet was surprised and shocked to find the hatred in his heart. Kurt lost his hatred in a hand-to-hand encounter with a German youth whom he was forced to kill on the battlefield. He learned then that there was nothing individual or personal in his hate, but that it was directed against an ideology, a menacing evil. His conclusions were undoubtedly those of the author, who could not find room in his heart for malice toward any man.

In 1918, Zane Grey met Helen Cody Wetmore, who had published in 1899 her own story of the life of Buffalo Bill, under the title of *The Last of the Great Scouts*. Grey had admired Buffalo Bill as he admired Buffalo Jones, and he was pleased when Mrs. Wetmore asked him to collaborate with her on the revision of the book for republication. He gladly complied with the request and in addition wrote several pages for insertion in the revised version, which was published by Grosset and Dunlap under the original title.

Zane Grey was writing more voluminously in those days, despite the active life he was leading. He made it a point to write something every day, if only notes. He turned out as much as 100,000 words a month—and all in longhand, for he preferred to write with pencil on lined paper, stacking up the finished pages in neat order as he worked.

He made extensive notes on the memorable trip into the wilderness of Tonto Basin with his son, Romer. These notes provided the material for two works: *Tales of Lonely Trails*, already mentioned, and *Zane Grey's Book of Camps and Trails*, written primarily for the benefit of tenderfoot campers the age of his son. The latter was published with a foreword by Franklin K. Mathiews, Chief Scout Librarian of the Boy Scouts of America, who praised the work highly as the kind of book that had long been needed and would not soon be equaled. Expressing his admiration for Zane Grey, Mr. Mathiews wrote: "From such a hunter, such a father, a boy learns the joys of the hunt and what it is to be a good sportsman in the wilderness. Man-to-man talk it is, imparted with tact, written with delicate touch and fine feeling, altogether free from sickly sentimentalism."

This was chiefly the story of Romer Grey. Other members of the party—R.C., the cowboy Joe Isbel, Lee and Al Doyle who served as guides, and Grey's friend Sievert Nielsen—were mentioned only incidentally, although each of these characters was a story in himself, especially Nielsen, the Norwegian sailor and adventurer.

In the course of Zane Grey's travels, he met many strange people under unusual circumstances. His acquaintance and subsequent friendship with Sievert Nielsen started with a letter that caught the author's attention as he was going through his fan mail one day. It was signed by an "S. Nielsen" who had just finished reading *Desert Gold*, Grey's romance of a lost gold mine. The story must have been extremely realistic to the Norwegian, who was convinced that the lost mine actually existed and, furthermore, that Grey could lead him directly to it. The letter was not written for the purpose of extolling the merits of the book, but rather to make a business proposition. Nielsen, who claimed to have had some experience as a prospector, stated that he was now ready to devote himself in earnest to the quest for gold. He wanted to accompany the author on an expedition to the fictitious mine and generously offered to split the proceeds, fifty-fifty!

Grey was half amused at the letter, but this stranger's naïveté and spirit of adventure struck his fancy. Acting on impulse, as he frequently did, he wrote a personal reply, explaining regretfully that the treasure of *Desert Gold* was purely imaginary, but that there was adventure, if not boundless wealth, to be found on the desert. He finished by inviting Nielsen to come to Avalon and visit him, and although the invitation was a sincere one, he was somewhat surprised at the promptness with which it was accepted.

Nielsen proved to be as forthright and refreshing as his letter. He was a large, brawny man with handsome Nordic features, light hair, tanned complexion, and steady gray eyes. Grey took an immediate liking to the man and was captivated by his yarns of world travel and adventure at sea. His seafaring days were over, he said; he now considered himself a prospector for gold, and already he had to his credit a number of lone expeditions into the desert of Lower California. He had never struck it rich, but he had learned some valuable things about prospecting and had lived through some exciting experiences.

He told Grey of an incident that had occurred when he was prospecting in the Sierra Madres alone. One night his burros disappeared; whether they were killed by mountain lions or simply strayed away from camp and were lost in the wilderness, he never knew. At any rate, he was left with a collection of valuable equipment and no means of transporting it back to the nearest point of civilization, roughly one hundred and fifty miles away. He could not bear the thought of parting with the more expensive items of his outfit, so he set out on foot, carrying as much as he could manage, and since he was already heavily weighted, took no food except a few biscuits and a canteen of water. He walked steadily, stopping every few hours to rest but never permitting himself to sleep, until at the end of three days and three nights he reached the nearest ranch.

The story would have been incredible to Grey if he had not seen the man in person and observed his powerful physique. Here was a man even more venturesome than himself, and with greater strength of endurance. A fast friendship soon grew up between the two men and they went on several expeditions together before Nielsen moved on to other adventures.

Nielsen was an asset to any expedition, for he was a man of calm courage, quick wit, and even disposition. After the Tonto Basin expedition, terminated so abruptly by the news of the sweeping epidemic of influenza, Nielsen and Grey began to lay plans for an exploratory expedition on their own.

Grey had long been intrigued by stories of Death Valley. He had studied its history dating from the time it was known by name. He knew that it was named as a result of the disaster that befell a Mormon caravan crossing it in their trek from Salt Lake to the newly-found gold fields of California. They had hoped that the route they adopted would prove a lucky shortcut. Had they known of the fate that lay in wait for them, they would have embarked as willingly on a deliberate expedition to Hades. Wandering and lost, choked with thirst, blinded by driving clouds of dust, crazed by the intense heat and the horrors of that never-ending series of sink-holes, they fell and perished. Out of a band of seventy, only two survived to tell the tale of the tragedy that had overtaken their comrades. From that day forward, the name of Death Valley struck fear into the hearts of the most daring of adventurers.

It was not that Grey was skeptical of the stories he had heard and read; it was simply his insatiable curiosity that compelled him to go and see for himself. Nielsen was of the same bent, and they agreed that they would cross the Valley together. There was none of the daredevil spirit about this adventure; they approached the project with awe and some apprehension, mingled with the grim determination to conquer rather than be conquered by this foreboding aspect of Nature.

They set out in the spring of 1919, traveling by train to Death Valley Junction, the nearest railway stop some fifty miles from the edge of the Valley. There they spent the evening talking to old prospectors who knew the desert and spoke familiarly of the ore deposits of silver, lead, zinc, copper—and gold—on the surface of the Valley. Nielsen bargained for pack mules and was up at dawn the next morning gathering together the necessary equipment.

While Nielsen attended to the packing, Grey went on an inspection tour of the borax mill of "twenty mule team" fame. It had been thirty years since the team of twenty mules had been used to haul borax ore up from the floor of the Valley. Hauling was now done by train, and the mill was kept running night and day, pulverizing and baking the ore as it was fed into the chutes. Grey was appalled at the sight of men spending their days in the choking dust of the mill, and by the foreman's remark that no man could endure the work in the mines for more than six months. He reflected that he was subjecting himself to this atmosphere voluntarily; that to him it was nothing more than a brief adventure. Yet to the laborers he met it presented no glamor, no variety; it was simply bread and butter. He was deeply moved by the experience.

"When I got out into the cool, clean desert air," he recorded, "I felt an immeasurable relief. And that relief made me thoughtful of the lives of men who labored, who were chained by necessity, by duty or habit, or by love, to the hard tasks of the world. It did not seem fair. These laborers of the borax mines and mills, like the stokers of ships, and coal-diggers, and blast-furnace hands —like thousands and millions of men, killed themselves outright or impaired their strength, and when they were gone or rendered useless others were found to take their places. . . . As the years go by my respect and reverence and wonder increase for these men of elemental lives, these horny-handed toilers with physical things, these uncomplaining users of brawn and bone, these giants who breast the elements, who till the earth and handle iron, who fight the natural forces with their bodies."

By midday the borax mill was lost to sight as Nielsen and Grey plodded up the gravelly slope to the "jump-off place" and passed through the gap between the Black Mountains and the well-named Funeral Range. The mountain pass was about three thousand feet above sea level, and pleasantly cool; but as the men started their difficult descent through loose, rain-washed gravel, they were aware of the contrast that awaited them, for Death Valley sank far below sea level and the temperature was known to range as high as 135 degrees. Grey felt the urgency of conserving energy for the ordeal ahead and he had to complain of the pace set by Nielsen, whose stride was much longer than that of his companion. Nielsen obligingly shortened his steps, but they had easily covered fifteen miles by sundown.

Suddenly a sharp turn in the canyon revealed a panorama that left even Nielsen speechless. The vista between two mountain ranges was that of a bottomless void, "a vast stark valley that seemed streaked and ridged and canyoned, an abyss into which veils of rain were dropping and over which broken clouds hung, pierced by red and gold rays." This was their first view of Death Valley.

After surveying the scene silently for some moments, Nielsen spoke to the mules and moved on. Grey, intent upon the changing color of the twilight hour, lagged behind to absorb all the weird unreality of the setting. The sinking sun left a red haze lingering over the valley, and beyond the fiery haze lay alternate patches of white borax flats and black unfathomable depths, reminiscent of Dante's Inferno.

When he caught up with Nielsen, he found the latter matter-of-factly going about the business of pitching camp for the night. Darkness had fallen and the desert breeze was cool. The silence was so intense that neither of the men felt like talking. They prepared and ate their supper with a minimum of conversation, then made their beds and went to sleep under the clouded, starless sky.

It was still cloudy and threatening the following morning when they broke camp, but as they proceeded the sky cleared and their spirits lifted. It was noon when they reached a warm stream known as Furnace Creek and stopped to rest on the bordering oasis. They found the water of the creek unfit for drinking purposes, and at a nearby spring a bleached skull half embedded in the sand gave mute evidence of the poisonous water that had lured at least one thirsty wanderer to his death. Climbing to the top of a ridge, Grey was able to command a better view into the depths of the canyon, "a smoky weird murky hell with the dull sun gleaming magenta-hued through the shifting pall of dust." He was most profoundly impressed by the manner in which "the gruesome and the beautiful, the tragic and the sublime, go hand in hand" in the desert.

Afternoon brought increasing heat and humidity and their camp that night, farther down the course of Furnace Creek, was swept by a warm gale that did not subside until dawn. In the clear, gleaming sunrise, they broke camp and moved on, continuing to follow the stream until they came unexpectedly upon some green alfalfa fields. Set in the midst of the green fields was a little cabin, where a lone rancher lived.

The rancher's name was Denton, and the strange coincidence of this meeting on the desert was the discovery that he was the brother of a guide Grey had known in Lower California. Denton lived in his small cabin and raised alfalfa for the mules of the borax miners, aided during certain seasons of the year by small groups of Shoshone Indians who camped nearby as long as there was work to be had, then moved on into the hills.

Why a man would choose to live out his days in seclusion in this lonely spot was not clear to Grey, but in the manner of the West he refrained from asking questions of a personal nature. He rather imagined that Denton, like himself, was irresistibly drawn to those lonely places from which other men shrank. He sensed this similarity in their makeup, at the same time realizing their fundamental difference, for although he was fascinated by the uninhabited wastelands of the earth and compelled again and again to revisit them, he had an equal need for human companionship that would never have permitted him to adjust happily to the life of a hermit.

Denton received his visitors hospitably and in answer to their questions offered complete, detailed information about the terrain, although it was obvious that speech did not come easily to him, for like all men of the desert he was more accustomed to silence than to conversation. When he learned of their intention he was reluctant to encourage them. It was not a venture to be undertaken lightly. He had seen others attempt it, ignorant of the torrid blasts that swept unrelentingly through the Valley and the hot summer nights when thermometers broke at 125 degrees. From his lonely outpost at the edge of the inferno, Denton had seen prospectors and adventurers set out on the journey at dawn, and he had watched them return at night, staggering blindly, babbling incoherently, their tongues, swollen and black, protruding between lips that were cracked and bleeding. Sometimes they were so crazed for want of water that he had to tie them down like mad steers and feed them a spoonful of water at a time, lest they kill themselves by drinking too deeply. It was true that some men withstood the heat better than others, but it required perfect lungs and heart and a strong reserve of energy, for the intense heat and the atmospheric pressure below sea level had the effect of drying up the blood and tissues. Men who were heavy meat-eaters or drinkers were doomed at the outset, Denton said.

Nielsen and Grey listened in respectful silence. They did not doubt Denton's information, but if it was volunteered with the hope of dissuading them it did not accomplish its purpose. Even the discovery of animal skeletons and a row of nameless desert graves near the oasis did not deflect them. They pitched camp on the oasis that night, conscious of the increasing heat unrelieved by any suggestion of a breeze. Grey was amazed to hear the musical trilling of frogs—the same sound that had lulled him to sleep in the Mexican jungle—and the note of a killdeer who, for some inscrutable reason, had forsaken his marshy habitat for the arid depths of Death Valley. He was even more amazed, the following day, to find delicate, fragile flowers blooming in the desert sand.

Breaking camp the next morning, they sought out Denton and told him they were prepared to start walking across the Valley. In dead earnest, the rancher tried to persuade them to give it up.

"The heat is not so bad, this time of year," he explained, "but there are other things. Poison gases, for example. And then there are sink-holes hidden by a layer of salt crust that will break through with a man's weight." He looked thoughtfully upon the massive body of Nielsen as he spoke these words. Then, looking anxiously at the sky, he warned them of the deceptive haze that intensified the glare rather than dulling it.

Nielsen and Grey took note of all his warnings, but their minds were made up and they set out with the determination to let caution temper their courage.

The salt crust of which Denton had spoken was indeed treacherous. It was a dirty yellow color, and it appeared solid enough but now and then it sounded hollow underfoot and the men stepped quickly over these spots. Ahead was an expanse of glistening white that looked like snow, and it was toward this dazzling plain that they were toiling. Grey had to stop and rest several times before they reached the plain, for the distance was greater than it appeared and he was again finding it difficult to keep abreast of Nielsen. He hated to admit fatigue, so instead of telling his companion that he had to rest, he simply said, "I want to take a few notes before we go any farther." Then, sitting on the alkali floor of the Valley, he would take out notebook and pencil with which to record his reactions and observations while he caught his second wind.

Arriving at the edge of the white plain, he found that no more such rest stops would be possible, for the glistening surface was even less solid than the stuff upon which they had been walking. Grey saw the white crust quiver under Nielsen's heavy boot and crumble with his weight, revealing beneath it a layer of a slimy yellow substance. He took a few steps and found that although he did not sink in as deeply as Nielsen, he did break through the surface and felt the earth tremble under his feet.

This was one of the sink-holes, without a doubt; and in all probability it led to more sink-holes. There was no way of predicting how much distance they would have to travel before they felt terra firma once more. Grey paused, but Nielsen admonished him that a man could easily sink through the surface if he stood in the same spot, but that if he proceeded quickly the danger would be much less.

Knowing that his friend spoke the truth, Grey retorted with a grim attempt at humor: "Lead the way, Nielsen. If it will hold you up, it will surely hold me. But if you go down, I can turn around and go back!"

Shouting with laughter, the fearless Norwegian stepped out over the perilous crust, and Grey, although conscious of the chill of fear along his spine, did not suit his words to action but boldly walked alongside his friend. If one went down they would both go down. Carefully watching their footing, wasting no time on distant looks ahead, they made their slow progress across the field of white. This, they had learned from Denton, was the lowest spot in this portion of the Valley, supposed to be at least two hundred feet below sea level.

It was like a river running through the center of the Valley—a river of shifting wet sands, with a thin crust that gave the appearance of a thin, treacherous coating of ice.

They were hours reaching the opposite bank of the river of salt, but they made it safely. There was scarcely time to catch their breaths, to sip from their canteens and mop their wet faces, before they plunged into a mud flat with broken, jagged crusts jutting upward, full of sharp drops and sudden pitfalls. They were not so conscious of danger here, but they were still not inclined to rest until they had reached the comparatively solid footing of loose gravel that sloped upward toward the mountains at the eastern rim of Death Valley.

They had come only seven miles, and already the sun was far past its zenith. It would be blazing directly into their faces on the trip back, and the effect on their vision might be disastrous. With this prospect in mind, they dared not linger long on the eastern slope, but turned their faces westward to retrace their steps.

Shimmering heat waves were rising from the floor of the desert and the glare of the dreaded crust of white was blinding. The upheavals of sharp salt crust were like fence pickets. Grey, who did not possess Nielsen's incredible endurance, became immensely weary. Now and then he fell forward, lacerating his hands on the stinging crust. His boots were wrecked, his clothing torn, and his shins battered and bleeding, but he did his best to keep from lagging behind.

Then suddenly when he thought he was on solid footing, the crust gave way beneath him and one foot plunged downward into a biting, acid liquid. In a flash, Nielsen was at his side pulling him back from the brink of the murky hole thus exposed by the break in the crust. For one horror-struck instant they stood peering down into the ghastly pit, and Nielsen broke the tense silence with an apt quotation: "Forty feet from hell!"

Without further misstep they crossed the white plain to the yellow salt flats beyond. This was not such rough going, but fatigue was rapidly overtaking them both, and mingled with the fatigue was a nervous exhaustion. Their breath came gaspingly; their clothing was wet with perspiration. The last hour was the slowest they had ever known.

And then their feet touched firm sand. Pebbles rolled under their boots, and the ground began gradually to rise. They flung themselves down and drank greedily from their canteens.

Back in camp at twilight, Grey rested in the shade and meditated upon the day's adventure in the Valley of Death and his own strange fascination for the place, despite its terrors. It was a place for man to face his soul, and because of its desolation and tragedy, it would seldom be visited by men. It was one of the lonely places of the earth that seemed to belong to him, by virtue of his own arduous efforts to seek them out.

Some day be would come back. But even as he made this promise to himself, a warm, suffocating blast of desert wind swept across the oasis camp and he longed for the contrast of a fresh ocean breeze. The cry of the killdeer overhead became the voice of the Lorelei and the cluster of far-off mountain peaks were the sails of a gallant ship.

The Cruise of the "Fisherman"

Zane Grey never completely abandoned a dream, though he frequently had to postpone the day of fulfillment. It was not until 1924 that his dream of a ship materialized. That autumn he went fishing off the coast of Nova Scotia and gained some publicity for his catch of a 758-pound tuna. Still full of excitement over his successful fishing jaunt, he stopped at Lunenberg and looked over the ships in the harbor, many of which were for sale. He had made up his mind to buy one and outfit it for his own deep-sea fishing, but the problem was to find a vessel that would fit both his ideal and his pocketbook.

There were many bargains to be had in former rum-runners, but Grey's principles on that score were so strong that he was forced to pass them by. "I would not have a bootlegger's vessel as a gift," he declared.

The *Marshal Foch* was for sale, and at a reasonable price. She was a fine three-masted schooner with an overall length of 190 feet and had a good reputation for seaworthiness and speed. Grey talked to the men who had sailed her and learned that she had crossed the

Atlantic twice, had made record runs between New York and Halifax, and—luckily for him—had never carried illicit cargo.

When the deal was completed he could hardly believe that the ship was his own, to sail where he pleased. His dream of a cruise to the South Seas was now a possibility.

He renamed the schooner *Fisherman*, and put a crew to work making the necessary changes preparatory to an extended tropic cruise. Captain Sid Boerstler, who was in charge of the work crew, estimated that the job would be completed in three months, which seemed to the new owner a long time to wait. Lest he become impatient, he planned to absent himself from the Nova Scotia harbor and cram the next months full of other activities.

He departed almost immediately for the West Coast, where he met his brother, R.C., and, with a small party of anglers, headed north to Oregon to fish in the Rogue River, which in the past two years had become one of Grey's favorite haunts. He was chagrined to discover that, although he had landed a giant tuna some weeks earlier—not without a fight, it was true—he could fish for steelhead day after day without landing so much as a five-pounder. R.C. had marvelous luck, and even the inexperienced lads who had come along to drive the trucks could boast of their catch, while native anglers assured them that this was the best season they had known in years. Things had reached a sorry state, indeed, when faithful George Takahashi looked up from his cooking and remarked candidly, "You awful rotten fisherman this trip."

Grey was inclined to agree with Takahashi; he had never known any angler to have such a run of bad luck.

But still he was determined not to quit, telling himself that "Every defeat is a stepping-stone to victory." His victory, when he finally achieved it at the end of two weeks of luckless casting, was a small one—a steelhead weighing no more than four pounds—but it broke the spell and led to bigger and better catches. One day yielded eight, another four, and another five, until on their last day he and R.C. were neck-and-neck in competition, R.C. with twenty-two, Grey with twenty-one. The contest was not decided until after sunset that day, when Grey, with R.C. coaching enthusiastically from the bank, landed an eight-pound steelhead to tie the score.

From this adventure, they moved on to southeastern Oregon for a hunting trip, and thence to Altadena, where Grey concentrated on writing, even though his mind was full of plans for the most ambitious cruise he had ever undertaken—and in his own ship.

Before leaving Nova Scotia, he had selected a sailing-master and crew, and their instructions were to meet the owner at Balboa, the western port on the Panama Canal. The *Fisherman* was ready to sail in December, which was a bad month on the Atlantic with heavy gales and high seas, but the schooner made its first port in Santiago without mishap, after twelve days of difficult sailing. Grey was kept informed by cable of the ship's progress from there to Jamaica and her subsequent departure for Colon, Panama. He began his own preparations to leave for the Canal Zone in time to meet her.

But the *Fisherman* was a victim of ill fortune, or ill management, for her master charted a dangerous course between close reefs and ran her aground on a small unknown Caribbean island. While the crew were busily engaged in attempts to back her off the reef, swarms of natives came alongside in canoes, hoping to loot the ship. It was a tense moment, and although the ship's master seemed unaware of the danger, Captain Sid Boerstler had his rifle at hand every minute in case trouble flared up. None of the savages were successful in coming aboard, and the ship got underway again, apparently none the worse for the mishap. In Colon, however, it was discovered that she had stripped her keel, and while she was in drydock for repair, there was a rapid exchange of cables that resulted in the discharge of the sailing-master. "Captain Sid" replaced him, at Grey's request, and in mid-January took the ship on to Colon, where Grey was to join them at the end of the month.

The ship lived up to his fondest dream. He was happy to find her in such good condition and to note the improvements that had been effected. New staterooms had been added, bringing the total to fourteen—eight above and six below deck. There were new quarters for the crew, an enlarged dining room, a new refrigerator plant, a dark-room for photography, and a special storeroom to accommodate their fishing tackle. There were three specially-constructed motor launches designed to battle high tides and rough seas and which combined all the best features of California, Florida, New Jersey, and Nova Scotia fishing launches.

In addition to Captain Sid and his crew, the party included R.C. and Romer, both anticipating the greatest adventure of their lives; Bob King, with whom Grey had fished in Florida; Jess Smith, Arizona cowboy with whom Grey had hunted in the Tonto Basin; Smith's wife, an artist who occupied herself making sketches of various scenes and incidents during the voyage; Chester Wortley, motion-picture cameraman from the Lasky studios; Captain Laurie Mitchell, the British sportsman;

137

Johnny Shields, a young friend of Romer's; Mrs. Phillips Carlin and Grey's secretary, Miss Millicent Smith. Last but not least was the cheerful little Japanese cook, George Takahashi, who was rapidly making himself indispensable to any Zane Grey expedition.

On January 30 the *Fisherman* sailed from Balboa. By evening land had disappeared from sight and on the second day out, heading southwest into the lonely Pacific waters, not another ship was sighted. The rolling motion of the ship was strange to Grey, and at night even the stars seemed not to be in their accustomed places. On the fourth day out, they struck calmer seas and waters that were too warm for a comfortable shower. Still there were no signs of life about them save for occasional leaping schools of blackfish and flocks of gulls that followed in the wake of the ship as if impelled by curiosity.

Captain Sid said they should be nearing Cocos Island, their first destination, and immediately there was a contest to determine who would be the first to sight land. It appeared most likely that one of the crew members would have the honor for they could clamber aloft to the crow's nest and on to the end of the topsail spar with no apparent difficulty, and they had the further advantage of being able to distinguish the deceptive trade-wind clouds from land, something that landlubbers could not easily do.

Grey, admiring the agility of a muscular seaman who climbed as easily as a monkey, and envying him the view that vantage point commanded, summoned his own courage and ascended to a point high above decks, where the dizzying motion of the ship was greatly magnified. He was stricken with fear and nausea, but he clung there stubbornly until he saw on the horizon a sharp black peak that could not possibly be an illusory cloud.

With his ringing cry of "Land ho!" excitement reigned on the deck below. They had come five hundred miles, following so true a course that they were now, according to Captain Sid, within thirty-five miles of the lone little island, a mere speck in the midst of the vast Pacific.

"Feel more better now," confessed Takahashi, as though he had feared they would never make it. Romer and his friend, Johnny, also appeared relieved, although they had been having the time of their lives trolling for dolphin, and had already hauled in a beautiful black-and-gold fellow weighing thirty pounds.

The boys were delighted at the sight of land, but as they drew nearer Cocos Island their glee knew no bounds, for here were schools of leaping tuna and an amazing variety of fish such as they had never seen before. They lost no time in baiting their lines and dropping them overboard as soon as Captain Sid gave the "drop anchor" order. Johnny immediately became engaged in battle with a four-foot shark and all the passengers gathered at the rail to watch the fun.

Grey detached himself from the group, feeling the demand for solitude that had always been a part of his nature. Gradually there was a relaxing of the tension he had built up during the months of hard work and careful planning for the expedition. Anxieties over the safety of the *Fisherman*, her crew and passengers, vague misgivings at the enormity of their undertaking, all melted away in the bright tropical moonlight as he sat in a secluded spot on deck, looking at the dim outline of the beach, listening to the muted roar of the surf, and inhaling the strange new fragrance borne on the gentle evening breeze. In this moment alone he found ample reward for his labors and the fulfillment of a dream he had been nurturing for more than thirty years.

There was a good reason for choosing Cocos Island as a setting for his first South Sea island adventure. He had read of it years ago in stories of the English pirate, Davis, and his band, who were supposed to have been the inspiration for Stevenson's *Treasure Island*. In fact, it was quite probable that Cocos Island provided the setting for the novel, for according to history, Davis took refuge there after his numerous raids on other ships and island settlements, and used it as his base of operations between voyages to the wealthy coast of Peru where he pillaged ruthlessly, then fled to his island stronghold to bury the accumulated treasure. Whether this vast fortune was ever removed from the island remains a mystery to this day.

Nor was Davis the only man who used this remote spot as a treasure island. More than a century later it was visited by a Captain Thompson, who carried a cargo of gold and jewels from Peru, entrusted to him for safe-keeping by a number of wealthy Spaniards who feared that their personal valuables would be stolen by looting soldiers in the revolution of 1820. Thompson buried the riches, estimated at that time to be worth more than twelve million dollars, on Cocos Island.

Later, hoping to regain the treasure, he joined with a band of pirates and narrowly escaped capture when the pirate chief Bonita was taken. Thompson showed up next in Newfoundland where, with his tales of buried treasure, he persuaded a number of adventurers to outfit a ship to go to Cocos Island, there to be led by Thompson himself to the secret cache. His death prevented fruition of the elaborate plans. But before he died, he drew a detailed map of the island, indicating the precise location

On May 8, 1936, he landed this world-record Tiger Shark. Hooked off Sydney, Australia, it weighed 1036 pounds.

Zane Grey wrote every one of his six million
published words in longhand.

of the treasure. With that map as guide, many expeditions of treasure hunters sailed to the island, and one group was known to be successful in uncovering gold and jewels valued at a hundred thousand dollars. Quarrels arose as to the division of the booty, and finally a member of the party named Keating made his getaway alone in a boat with the entire fortune, after outwitting his fellows. What became of Keating and his precious cargo was never known.

There were those who believed that this was only a small part of the buried treasure, and expeditions to the island did not cease. In 1924, less than a year before the *Fisherman* dropped anchor off Cocos Island, a treasure-hunting ship had been anchored there. Its passengers and crew had spent weeks searching the island, but with no success.

There was not a soul aboard the *Fisherman* who could have been persuaded to abandon fishing in favor of treasure-hunting, though the island's history intrigued them. Viewing the island by daylight, Grey was impressed by the number of hiding-places it afforded, for the coast was rugged and broken; its sheer cliffs rising up from the sea were draped with matted tangles of moss that concealed, or half-concealed, many a rocky cavern which would have been extremely difficult of access.

The launches were lowered bright and early the first morning and the big fishing adventure began. Romer and Johnny went with Captain Mitchell in the smaller boat, while Grey and his brother got in the larger one, piloted by Bob King. Chester, the cameraman, in the third boat, hovered about in hopes of getting some good action shots.

There was action a-plenty. Not knowing the nature or size of the fish in those waters, Grey and R.C. started off with light tackle. Within a few minutes they learned their error. First R.C., then Grey, hooked a heavy fish only to see it run rapidly out to sea and break the line. Immediately they switched to heavy tackle, whereupon Grey's first strike was not a fish, but a bird. The frigate-birds in this wild and lonely spot were both curious and hungry. They followed close after the fishermen's boat and repeatedly swooped down to snatch away the cut-fish bait. One of them, in attempting to fly away with the bait, caught his beak on the hook and began to fight it, while his fellows, realizing there was some danger involved, set up a great squawking and came to his res-cue. Slowly, carefully, Grey reeled him in, while Chester, following in the camera boat, was busy photo-graphing the graceful bird. At last the bird was caught; Grey removed the hook from his beak and set him free. But the bird had not learned his lesson. He rejoined the flock in attacking the bait as wildly as before. The birds proved such a nuisance that fishing was impossible until they became more accustomed to the sight of the boat.

R.C., with typical luck, was the first to land a fish—a handsome yellowtail weighing twenty pounds. His luck, however, was insignificant compared to that of Johnny and Romer. They had wandered away from Cocos Island to a smaller one nearby that turned out to be a bird rock, with hundreds of boobies sailing in the air and hundreds of nests visible on the rocky cliff overlooking the channel. These birds apparently had offered the fish no competition for bait, for the boys hauled in a dozen fish, all good-sized, and all of a purplish hue, though they were of different species. Grey could positively iden-tify the crevalle, of which there were nine, by their exotic coloring of pale blue and purple; the others were questionable. But there was no question that the boys had seen sharks and given them a good battle. They were re-ported to be huge yellow creatures with gleaming silver fins, swift as lightning and twice as sinister.

The more experienced men felt their blood chill at the thought, but nothing short of darkness or extreme hunger could stop the dauntless young anglers. They were out again the next morning, soon after a drizzly gray dawn, unmindful of high wind and waves. From the deck, Grey watched with mingled pride and apprehension as Romer stood up in the boat, rifle in position, shooting at sharks while Johnny reeled in a large yellowtail.

Later in the day Grey had his first encounter with one of those sharks and found himself the loser, with nothing but a broken line to show for the experience. It turned out to be an off-day for R.C., too, so they agreed to spend the day exploring the island. They went ashore when they found an inviting strip of white beach with coconut palms set back against the jungle's fringe and a clear stream crossing it to empty into that portion of the sea which was known as Wreck Bay.

The boys joined them on the beach and together they discovered the remains of a shack where, according to legend, a treasure-seeker had once lived alone and from which he had disappeared without a trace. Other evidences of the island's history were found later when the whole party came ashore to explore. Names of pirates, of sailors and treasure-hunters, and of ships were carved in the rocks, sometimes with accompanying dates, as far back as 1817. Some were still clear and distinct; others were half effaced by the effects of weather and surf. There was even a cache of dynamite left by adventurers who presumably had given up their quest and did not want to undergo the needless risk of carrying explosives on the homeward voyage. Quite by accident they came upon the remains of a ship that had been wrecked on the rocks and although it was impossible to determine the origin of the sunken vessel, it was assumed to be one of the Spanish galleons of the pirate Morgan, for there was no history of any recent wreckage in the vicinity of the island.

Romer and Johnny, bursting with youthful energy and curiosity, followed the little stream for a short distance into the jungle and brought back wild tales of green spiders, birds with golden plumage, wild pigs, and numerous tracks they had been unable to identify. Grey did not bother to penetrate the jungle to corroborate their stories, for he found that he was quite content to loaf along the beach observing the jungle foliage, the exotic wild flowers, the distant waterfall, and the ever-present birds soaring above.

On the following day, however, the beauty of Wreck Bay was wasted on him, for the purple waters were alive with fish: crevalle, yellowtail, turbot—and sharks. There were battles with birds as well as with sharks, for the birds hovered near eager to steal bait, and the sharks whose lurking shadows were visible in the clear shallow waters were ever ready to attack a fish when it was hooked, making it necessary for the anglers to reel in quickly to avoid losing their fish. Even then the great yellow sharks would follow their quarry up to the side of the boat, flashing by swiftly, sometimes splashing water on the occupants, sometimes striking the boat itself with a blow that made it rock.

Attracted by the blood of fish that had been hooked or gaffed, sharks came from every direction to follow after the boat. The fishermen could look down and see them clearly, huge creatures measuring twelve feet and more. Angered by their interference, Grey declared war on them and after hard fighting brought in three, the largest weighing in the neighborhood of 250 pounds. Bob King cut up the carcass and rolled it overboard into the water. Instantly cannibal sharks appeared from nowhere, flashed past the boat and engaged in battle over their fallen comrade, while the men in the boat watched in horrified fascination through the crystal-clear water. This ghastly battle made it clear to Grey that fishing in tropic seas could never be the sport that it was in safer waters where game fish were sufficiently free from fear to play close to the surface. Yet there were thousands more fish in these waters than Grey or R.C. had dreamed.

Romer, vowing that a few sharks could not spoil his fun, went out the next day and returned with a strange, dark-colored fish which he could not identify although he could honestly attest it was "a fighter." His father was amazed and delighted to discover that Romer had caught a wahoo. He had seen few of the species; in fact, he was the only angler ever known to have caught one at Long Key, where they were extremely rare.

Romer's wahoo was extraordinarily large for the species and it revived Grey's waning incentive to outwit the sharks in the pursuit of game fish. He went out in the launch with Romer that afternoon, while R.C. set off in another boat equipped with heavy swordfish tackle. He, too, had absorbed some of the youthful optimism radiated by the younger generation and his excitement was soon equal to Romer's, for he ran straight into a school of leaping yellow-fin tuna, one of which he landed very quickly.

In the other boat Romer was kept busy with strike after strike, but in spite of his valiant efforts he could not whip those heavy, swift-moving tuna. When the boy had reached the fatigue point, his father suggested turning back to see how R.C. was doing.

They found him putting the finishing touches on a victory over a twelve-foot shark. R.C. hauled the monster in alongside the launch and a sailor who had been standing in wait with a long spear stabbed it. R.C. was triumphant, but still filled with fury at the sharks for spoiling his sport. It seemed that there were ten sharks to one yellow-fin and if he were to catch any of the latter he would first have to rid the surrounding waters of sharks, of which he estimated there were an easy million in the immediate vicinity.

Grey, whose tackle had given out, turned his attention to photographing birds diving for fish. Besides the frigate-birds that had been annoying his bait, there were eagles, fish-hawks, kingfishers, gulls, terns, and the most expert of divers, the boobies. He was so entranced by the clean, graceful sweep of their wings and their swift descent to the water's surface that he missed the first scene of the drama being enacted from R.C.'s boat.

His first inkling of anything unusual came with the realization that Bob King, who accompanied R.C., was shouting hoarsely and waving his arms. From his position Grey was unable to discern the cause for excitement so he promptly turned about and drew closer until he could see dull flashes of yellow beneath the water's surface. R.C.'s rod was bent and he was exerting all his strength on the fighting tuna. Bob King reached for the leader and pulled mightily.

Suddenly the water broke wide open and with violent splashing the tuna's nose appeared, then his gills—and then, amazingly, the broad head and vicious jaws of a shark. R.C. was hauling in two fish, not one, for the shark had attacked the hooked tuna and swallowed him, all but his head!

The battle for the tuna waged relentlessly, with great churning of the waters to indicate that other sharks were following along, ready to close in and share in the kill. Bob King, determined not to let the sharks get away with it, gave a powerful pull on the leader, then suddenly fell backward into the launch as the shark's jaws snapped shut, leaving only the head of the tuna dangling on the line.

As the agitated water quieted it was possible to see beneath the surface at least a dozen large sharks, ranging possibly from six hundred to eight hundred pounds. Bob lured them to the surface with the bloody head of the tuna and they approached so near the boat that he was able to stick his spear into their heads. It was a gruesome, fascinating spectacle.

After dinner that night Romer was still recounting the incredible happenings of the day, but his father lacked zest for the adventure. Danger had never before given him pause, and he reflected that this excursion was different, for it was not merely a question of guarding his own life in a perilous situation; he was charged with the responsibility for a number of lives dearer to him than his own. The thought of what might happen if one or more sharks should attack a boat occupied by Romer and his exuberant friend, Johnny, was not a pleasant one, nor was it too far-fetched. There were known instances of boats caving in and sinking under shark attacks. The launches, with their air-tight compartments, were supposed to be unsinkable, but Grey was unwilling to flirt with danger on this expedition, particularly in view of the fact that they were far off the main highways of the Pacific, in a hopeless position as far as rescue by other ships was concerned.

With all these factors weighing heavily on his mind, he called a "council of war" to admonish the entire party —passengers and crew alike—to exercise extreme caution. He advised the use of heavy tackle and forbade the risky practice of gaffing sharks, giving strict orders that they be shot or speared instead. Even then he was not free from uneasiness. In his heart he was anxious to move on to the Galápagos, leaving the sharks of Cocos Island far behind, but rather than dampen the spirits of the party he consented to tarry a few days more.

The outstanding performance of those last days was given by Jess Smith, the Arizona cowboy who had never seen salt water before and held a fishing-rod much as he would have held a rifle. Whether it was beginner's luck, or stubbornness, or Jess's powerful muscles that deserved credit, he succeeded in landing a hundred-pound yellow-fin while the rest of the party, including Grey and Smith's wife, watched from the deck of the *Fisherman*. It was a breath-taking battle, and Grey was as tense as Mrs. Smith, though for a different reason: Jess was using one of Grey's favorite rods and was well on his way to wrecking it. While he shouted instructions to Jess relative to the proper handling of good equipment, Mrs. Smith was screaming at her husband not to fall overboard to save "an old fishing-pole." Meanwhile she was trying feverishly to photograph Jess and sketch him at the same time, with no notable success in either undertaking.

With advice and encouragement from all quarters, Jess hauled in his fish and George Takahashi gaffed it. It was brought up on deck for all to see—a beautiful varicolored creature predominantly silver and gold, black and purple, far more striking than the blue tuna Grey had caught off the coast of Nova Scotia the preceding autumn.

While the crowd gathered around to congratulate the triumphant, disheveled Jess, Grey looked ruefully upon his ruined rod.

"Serves you right," murmured Captain Sid, in amiable criticism. "You should know better than to lend good tackle!"

It was true, as Captain Sid remarked, that Romer and Johnny alone had wrecked enough tackle "to outfit a fishing village," and Grey quickly put aside any thought of the mere loss of one more rod as he entered into the ensuing celebration as wholeheartedly as the others— with the possible exception of Jess's wife who was practically delirious with pride.

After another day ashore, the party prepared to depart from Cocos Island, setting sail that evening in moonlight as bright as day; indeed, there was little distinction between day and night, for the moon was shining brightly before the last rays of the sun had disappeared. It was with some relief that Grey stood watching the receding cliffs of the magic island, for he had never felt comfortable in the shark-infested waters, though the island itself had a romantic charm. Undoubtedly the treasure was still hidden there; Grey was intuitively convinced of its presence. Nothing could have induced him to waste time searching for it, for he was certain that if it was ever found at all, it would be quite by accident, and he uttered the fervent hope that the discovery would fall to the lot of some "honest, needy fisherman."

Marchena Island, the first of the Galápagos Archipelago to reach their eyes, was a welcome sight after four hundred miles of placid sea with nothing to break the monotony except the occasional appearance of a school of dolphin or porpoises. There were flying-fish, too, and leaping tuna of a variety Grey identified as blue-fin.

As they passed by the first four islands of the Galápagos group, Grey was reminded of the barren reaches of Arizona desert with which he was so familiar. These were typical of the desert isles of romantic fiction, but were known to Grey through his many readings of Darwin's factual account of the *Voyage of H.M.S. Beagle* and Beebe's recent volume, *Galapagos, World's End*. The islands along the horizon assuredly gave the appearance of "world's end," with jutting volcanic peaks, barren desert, and sparse vegetation. There were many stories of shipwreck and pirate hideouts woven around this formidable archipelago.

Santa Cruz, as they approached it, was marked by volcanic peaks, black against the sky, with veins of red lava. The shore was made up of contrasting smooth beaches and clusters of enormous jagged rocks, and what vegetation was visible appeared to be a cactus growth. Grey knew that the island had never been explored, and later, after the *Fisherman* had dropped anchor in Conway Bay, he went ashore and learned the reason. The slopes rising upward from the sea were covered by impenetrable jungle, with matted vines concealing the rough lava formation of the ground so that he could not see where he was walking. This, combined with the equatorial heat and the nuisance of desert flies, discouraged exploration. However, there was enough of interest on the sandy beaches to absorb him: marine iguanas, somewhat similar to alligators, but apparently not at all dangerous; red and gold crabs scuttling along the rocks; fur-bearing seals; a variety of birds; and a number of tortoises, which accounted for the archipelago's former name, "Islands of the Tortoises."

Even more interesting was the variety of fishes abounding in the nearby waters, and the beauty of it was that there were few sharks to molest them, although sharks were sometimes seen at night flocking about the ship. The boys shot at them, and one twelve-foot creature, when hit, lunged against the ship with a reverberating whack. Nevertheless, they never proved a menace to daytime fishing as had been the case at Cocos Island.

There were wahoo, albacore, and dolphin in abundance. It was in Conway Bay that Grey caught a five-and-a-half-foot dolphin weighing fifty-one pounds, the largest dolphin he had ever seen and a world's record, so far as anyone could ascertain. R.C. caught a wahoo nearly as large as the one Romer hooked at Cocos Island and on another occasion he hauled in a sizable needle-fish that flopped over once in the launch and sank his sharp, needle-like jaws into Bob King's leg.

Occasionally Grey caught glimpses of giant rays, similar to those of the Gulf Stream but much larger. There was no reason for catching them, but there was a great contest to photograph them. This should have been easy, for the huge bat-like creatures measured as large as fifteen feet in diameter, with a probable weight of fifteen hundred pounds or more, but they appeared so unexpectedly and disappeared so quickly that it required constant vigil and ready cameras to get a good shot. A motion picture would have been a great prize, for the rays moved in a curious manner, appearing to be half-bird and half-fish as they rolled in the water and flapped their "wings."

R.C., in his determination to photograph one, hooked it from his launch and was towed miles out to sea before he could bring it in. He was gone so long that his brother, not knowing the reason, became anxious and was ready to set out in search of him when the missing launch appeared, towing the giant ray.

"I hated to kill him," R.C. apologized, "but that's what you have to do if you expect to photograph them or learn anything about them."

From this remark it was obvious that R.C. felt as his brother did, that the major purpose of the expedition was not to catch as many fish as possible, but to explore all phases of life in that sector of the Pacific and learn as much as possible about it. Even Romer was impressed by the opportunity to see strange new things and the obligation to report them accurately. He was an alert observer and possessed such a zestful manner in story-telling that his father was convinced that the boy was a born writer.

After a few days at Conway Bay, the *Fisherman* moved on to Darwin Bay off Tower Island, about eight hours distant. This island, formerly named "Nightmare Island" by Spanish seamen, was also a lava formation, and the bay itself was the crater of an extinct volcano. The stark appearance of the island, as well as the ominous roar of the surf against the dark rocks, explained to Grey the reason underlying the Spanish name given it. In the days that followed, it proved a nightmare to him as well, but for a very different reason.

Here, in contrast to the peaceful aspect of the myriads of tame swallows and gulls sailing overhead, were dark waters concealing sharks of greater size and ferocity than any of those around Cocos Island. This discovery was both alarming and discouraging. Grey was convinced that his entire South Pacific adventure was to be filled with the nightmare of man-eating sharks—for these black monsters, unlike the lighter ones of Cocos Island, were without a doubt man-eaters and could have swallowed a fisherman at one gulp, given the opportunity. Since that opportunity was not granted them, they contented themselves with plaguing the fishermen and robbing their lines.

One day, when Grey was doing battle with a six-foot wahoo, his fish leaped suddenly into midair, followed by a leaping giant of a shark, all of fifteen feet in length. Grey's loss was the shark's gain, and he stood in open-mouthed horror at the viciousness of this brute, leaping out of the sea to attack his prey. If Grey was horrified, his brother was infuriated, for once more R.C. had been on the verge of hauling in a large tuna when a shark appeared and devoured the body of the fish, leaving only the head for R.C.

R.C. swore he would not give up without a fight, and true to his word, he went to work and caught three sharks in rapid succession, all of them huge, ranging from three hundred to five hundred pounds in weight. Grey joined the grim crusade, but with no such luck as his brother's, for every time he hooked a shark, it chewed through the heavy copper-wire leader and got away.

More fearful than the shark menace was an unexpected storm that hit Darwin Bay in the middle of the night. The *Fisherman*, which was anchored perilously near the rocks for such seas, was buffeted and pitched about, while the small boats bobbed up and down like corks, now and again striking against the schooner's side. For a time there was a question of the advisability of putting out to sea, a safe distance from the rocky coast, leaving the boats behind, but the suggestion was vetoed for such a course would have left them without lifeboats should disaster strike the *Fisherman*. Nothing remained but to wait and hope that the gale would spend itself—which it did in the early hours of morning.

As soon as the sea was calm, the anchor was hoisted and the *Fisherman* set sail for the Perlas Islands off the Panama coast and lying about eight hundred miles to the northeast of the Galápagos. As far as Grey knew, they were headed for a fisherman's paradise. It was as well that he did not know they were heading straight toward what he later acknowledged was "the most harrowing experience of my life."

After three days of pleasant sailing, during which Grey and his party had spent many an exciting hour photographing leaping sperm whale of "Moby Dick" fame, the *Fisherman* ran into a squall during the night. Rain came down in torrents. Grey was awakened by the deluge, for the wind was blowing it in sheets through his open windows. Wide awake in an instant, he closed the windows, dressed quickly, and went out on deck to view the storm, relieved at the thought that they were far out in mid-ocean, safe from the danger of being dashed against a rocky coast.

Just as he was silently giving thanks that they were far away from the formidable Galápagos, he became conscious of the voices of the crew, shouting out in the darkness with tones that suggested alarm. Simultaneously he was struck down by a wind-driven wall of water. Struggling to his feet, he felt his way back to his stateroom to don boots and slicker, then carefully inched his way along the deck until, in the inky blackness, he could discern the mate at the wheel.

They could scarcely make themselves heard above the roar of the storm and the cracking of the sails, but Grey caught the mate's words: "Sighted steamer . . . can't see now . . ." and grasped their horrible significance.

This was a peril far greater than rocky reefs, for at the whim of a storm, two vessels might be hurled together without a moment's warning, without a chance of warding off the dual disaster. In all his life, Zane Grey had never felt the cold fear that gripped his body with that realization. For a moment he could not move; then silently he turned from the mate and edged his way along the rail, peering out into the night.

It was futile to attempt to pierce the void beyond. Grey realized that when he discovered that he could not even see the length of his own ship; even her lights showed with ghostly dimness through the heavy downpour. She was rocking and straining against the storm, completely at its mercy.

He turned back to rejoin the mate and was surprised, and somewhat comforted to find Captain Sid at the wheel. At the sound of Grey's voice, the skipper shouted out with cheery reassurance, "Only a squall!"

"But the steamer!" Grey shouted back. "The mate told me . . ." The wind snatched the words from his lips.

For a brief instant the skipper's eyes met his. "That's a chance we have to take," he replied grimly.

Out of the darkness the mate reappeared and took his place beside the captain. Together they strained at the wheel and no more words were spoken.

Grey returned to the rail, alone with his paralyzing terror and bitter remorse. In all his dreams of sailing a beautiful ship into unknown seas he had never visualized such a fate as this. He had always pictured the ship riding smoothly over placid sunlit waters, her white sails outlined against a cloudless sky. The image of this hour's stark reality had never crossed his mind, nor had he ever

considered the possibility of innocent lives being sacrificed because of his foolish dream.

With a renewed sense of obligation to those who put
their confidence in him—unjustified as he now felt it to
be—he gained control of himself and determined to do
the only thing he could possibly do for those aboard his
ship. Clinging to the rail, he traversed the length of the
deck and took his place beside the lookout at the bow,
straining his eyes in a desperate endeavor to penetrate
the murky blackness.

The lookout was a Nova Scotian who had spent many
years at sea, and though they scarcely spoke to one another Grey was constantly aware of his stalwart presence. There was an air of composure about the man that
certainly did not come from ignorance of the invisible
threat, and Grey reflected that the sailor, like most Nova
Scotia fishermen, probably had deeply-rooted religious
convictions that gave him strength in these crises. Grey
was aware then that his own religion, though simple and
sincere, had not prepared him for anything like this. He
felt an overpowering urge to confide in the silent man
beside him, to partake somehow of his quiet courage.
Without taking his eyes from the heaving sea, he gave
voice to his innermost fears and deepest emotions, surprised at the ease with which the words rose to his lips
and at the feeling of diminishing tension as he spoke.
Probably half the words were drowned by the roaring
sea and the flapping sails, but Grey knew that the sailor
understood their substance when, after an interval of
thoughtful silence, he made his reply.

"Men who go down to the sea in ships," he said
quietly, "must be prepared."

The words had a calming effect on Grey's troubled
spirit, and at the same time recalled to him his own

philosophy of the divine spark that elevates primitive man to heights of nobility in the face of a crisis. His faith was strengthened.

Daybreak lent a nightmarish quality to the memory of the night's vigil on the bow as the dull gray light from the overcast skies disclosed no sign of another ship on the turbulent sea. They had passed the phantom steamer in the darkness—by how close a margin they would never know.

In the bright days of clear sailing that followed, the sharp terror of the experience gradually dimmed in Grey's mind but its imprint was left on his character. From a simple seafaring man he had learned a lesson that remained with him through life. He knew that he would always have his dreams, but never again would he permit them to bear him too far from the realm of reality.

A Home in the West

Scarcely had the *Fisherman* dropped anchor in home port before plans were brewing for another expedition into the South Seas. The first cruise had been a glorious adventure, ending with the homeward voyage up the West Coast from Panama Bay, with stopovers at Zihuatanejo Bay, with its picturesque village of friendly natives and its fine prospects for sailfish and marlin, and in San Lucas Bay off Lower California, which had proved to be a veritable fisherman's paradise despite the competition of commercial fishing vessels.

There were scenes that Grey definitely wanted to revisit. Among them was Pedro Gonzales Island, in the Perlas Archipelago, for although his luck had not been good there he was convinced that his native informant was telling the truth when he said that swordfish were usually plentiful, but that the Zane Grey party had arrived at the wrong season. There had been enough amberjack and redsnapper to provide sport, but not the keenest kind of sport, for they were too numerous; redsnappers by the thousands followed after the boat. There were sharks about the island, too, though Grey did not see many and caught none; but one of the native pearldivers told him that to his knowledge six of the divers had been eaten by sharks.

He knew that he would some day return to Zihuatanejo, not only because of the abundance of sailfish in nearby waters but because of the charm of the little Mexican village with its thatched houses and quiet streets where dogs, parrots, tame deer, pigs, and little children all played happily. The people there had been gracious and friendly, and Grey was surprised to find that they were white; possibly these fair-skinned, fine-featured villagers were direct descendants of Cortez' conquistadores and had kept themselves a group apart, without mingling with native Indian tribes. They had appeared genuinely sorry to see Grey depart, and he confessed to feeling "the thrill and pride of the explorer, the discoverer of an enchanted land."

Fortunately it would not be difficult to take an occasional short jaunt to the relatively nearby waters of San Lucas Bay in the Gulf of Lower California, where yellow-fin tuna ran in schools. Grey marveled at their stupidity, for they had not yet learned that these were the haunts of the large fishing fleets from San Diego and San Pedro. Blue-fin tuna had learned the lesson long ago and had moved to unknown distant waters. Albacore, likewise, were quick to recognize the human menace and betake themselves to safer spots; one season they were to be seen around Catalina Island in great numbers, the next season they were mysteriously gone. But the yellow-fin fell for the same old bait, year after year, in unconscious mass suicide. Grey had caught eight of them in one day at San Lucas, and then quit because he had broken all his lines, the rod-socket in his chair, and finally the chair itself. Another day he had hauled in six, ranging in weight from 135 to 215 pounds. Even Romer had been able to boast of a 184-pound tuna, and others smaller.

Actually the great attraction in the San Lucas vicinity so far as Grey was concerned, was the presence of marlin. He had seen one of the market fishing craft haul in a monster of a black marlin, weighing 690 pounds. He had not caught any himself, but he had followed with some excitement his brother's battle with a 170-pound striped marlin, and exulted over R.C.'s victory.

There were all kinds of memories of the fish that had been caught and the fish that got away. Grey remembered with special bitterness the famous black marlin of Zihuatanejo Bay. He had fought it for four and a half hours, until his hands were blistered and lacerated, his breathing was painful in his chest, and he was about to drop from exhaustion. Then, just as the marlin showed signs of fatigue, the line broke. To counteract that was the successful battle with a sailfish—doubly successful because when the fish surrendered, after making forty-three magnificent leaps into the air, Grey discovered that he had not only a beautiful sailfish specimen but a motion-picture record of the catch, for Chester had been grinding away all the while as he followed in R.C.'s boat. There were proud recollections of Romer's fishing prowess: his 65-pound rock bass caught in San Lucas Bay, the handsome blue-and-silver "rooster fish" he caught at Zihuatanejo, his two large yellow-fins, to say nothing of the many he fought valiantly and lost.

R.C. had a strange memory of catching one fish and losing another—when both were attached to the same line. This amazing incident occurred at Zihuatanejo, when R.C. hooked a fighting sailfish and another one, following along with the possible intention of liberating its mate, became entangled in the line. The irony was that the tangled fish was pulled in while the other one got safely away. Among other memories, R.C. had one of catching a dead tuna in San Lucas Bay. He had been fighting it for some minutes when he felt a peculiar tug on the line, as if his quarry might have been attacked by a shark, except that the pull was accompanied by an odd rotary motion. Suddenly the heavy drag on his line ceased; he reeled in his tuna, to find it covered with encircling scars that give unmistakable evidence of death in the tentacles of an octopus.

Everyone remembered the day in San Lucas Bay when all hands concerted efforts in an attempt to catch a whale shark. They had hooked it from one of the launches and were towed for miles out to sea, while other members of the party hurried back to the *Fisherman* for additional equipment: lengths of long, heavy rope; rifles, harpoons, and spears. After spending almost the entire day in this deadly project, the shark dived suddenly downward to a depth of more than 1500 feet, as indicated by the knots on the spliced rope-lengths. When the rope gave out there was nothing to do but acknowledge defeat, bitter though it was.

There were memories of special days during the cruise: the day the ship's whistles shrieked in celebration of crossing the Equator; the day they sighted the first steamer after many weeks on the high seas; the day of their first thrilling glimpse of the mountains of Lower California; the day they sighted the active volcano on San Salvador. There were countless recollections of the strange life at sea: of phosphorescent seas at night, and waters that glowed blood-red by day; the zone of swimming snakes, thirty miles from the Costa Rica coast, and the zone of turtles, swimming along with birds riding on their backs; the boobie that hitchhiked a ride on the *Fisherman*, sitting contentedly on the rail for hours before taking to the air again; the whales and dolphin that followed in the wake of the ship, leaping in play. There were memories of the camaraderie on shipboard; of the practical jokes played by Romer and Johnny when they should have been studying; of the remarks elicited by R.C.'s pale-green complexion as the *Fisherman* passed through stormy seas; of the friendly rivalry among the fishermen, and the cheery philosophy of Takahashi.

Besides all this, there was much tangible evidence of the success of the expedition, for souvenirs had been gathered at every port. Besides the usual rocks, seashells, native baskets and leatherwork, there were live souvenirs, for everyone aboard had bought parrots or parrakeets in Zihuatanejo, not to mention Grey's pet macaw, a few tame deer, Mexican turkeys, squirrels, and an odd animal purported to be an anteater, though more probably a species of Mexican raccoon, who went to a watery grave because of his proclivity for scrambling along the ship's rail. With this menagerie, plus the ship's cats that had joined the company in Balboa, there was no lack of entertainment on rainy days.

Best of all was the splendid collection of photographs brought back by the party. There were motion pictures taken by Chester on all the most exciting occasions of the voyage, supplemented by "stills" of inestimable value. To Grey's immense pride, they had been successful in taking the only known photographs of leaping sperm whales, and numbered among the collection of whale pictures a rare and beautiful sight of two whales' tails, one white and one black, protruding from the water as the two monsters made their downward plunges.

It was enough to encourage further ventures. Meanwhile, Grey had a busy year ahead of him, with notes of the expedition to be reworked for publication, photographs to sort and label, a novel to write, the summer fishing at Avalon, and plans to explore the length of Oregon's Rogue River in the fall. After that he could return to the Pacific—possibly even sail to New Zealand. Meanwhile it was good to be home.

Home for Zane Grey was "a place for love and comfort, a place of sweet rest." Long ago the little cottage at Lackawaxen had been left behind, although for sentimental reasons he could not find it in his heart to sell it. It was good to keep it as a reminder of the years before his rise to fame. He would go back, some day. But in the meantime the Greys had moved from place to place, seeking an ideal location to suit the whole family.

Through the years Grey gradually accumulated various properties for various reasons, most of them sentimental if he had stopped to analyze his feelings. There were the two ranches in Arizona's Tonto Basin, for example. After the memorable trip to Nonnezoshe with John Wetherill, he had set his heart upon a home in the West, and this seemed the ideal setting. This was the country that provided the background for several of his stories, notably *Under the Tonto Rim* and *The Rainbow Trail*. It was also the place where he became acquainted with the beautiful horses that were later to take an important place in his affections and in his novels. Everyone who read *Riders of the Purple Sage*—and they surely numbered upwards of a million—admired the horses, Night and Black Star and Blanco Sol, and knew that the writer who portrayed them so vividly was a true lover of horses. And so he was. During his sojourn in the Tonto Basin, he had become so attached to them that he was determined to buy them and take them back

East with him. This he did, to his great regret, for he learned that these sturdy animals could withstand desert life but they could not adjust to Eastern climate. Black Star and Blanco Sol died at Lackawaxen, and Night was shipped back to Arizona, lest the same fate should befall him. The moment Night alighted on his native soil, he was a different horse. All the old spirit returned to him as if by magic, and Grey, to whom the scene was poignantly touching, resolved never again to remove a Western horse from his original habitat. So he purchased land where Night, and more recently acquired horses, could range happily between hunting trips. As it turned out, Grey never lived on either of the Arizona ranches, but used them as hunting lodges and stayed there a month or two every year, hunting and riding through the forests of silver spruce and green pine, living in the open with ranch hands and fellow hunters.

Grey found that the ocean meant as much to him as the desert, though in a different sense. He was intrigued by its changing moods, its peaceful calm and its hidden dangers. That was one reason for his keen enjoyment of deep-sea fishing, for he longed to explore the limitless expanse of sea that stretched off to the horizon. He and R.C. had their greatest fishing adventures at Catalina Island, and there at Avalon Grey built an adobe home where the entire family could live. This, however, was used only during the summer months while he and R.C.— and, later, Romer—cruised that portion of the Pacific in quest of broadbill swordfish.

As a contrast to deep-sea fishing, there were occasional jaunts along inland waters for fresh-water fish. Grey and his brother found that they kept going back to the Rogue River in Oregon for trout fishing. Even while they were on their Pacific cruise, they talked of the steelhead in the Rogue River and wondered why it was that they longed to return to the mountain stream. Grey at last found the explanation: It was like home to them. They were accustomed to fresh-water fishing, from their boyhood days in Ohio and Pennsylvania. The ocean, while new and thrilling, was not their natural element. It challenged and uplifted, but it did not give them the comfortable feeling they had wading in rocky, bubbling streams casting for trout. The unbroken expanse of sea was strange to them, hard on their eyes, and they found that the Rogue River, with its contrasting green walls of forest on either side and distant mountain peaks towering above, was restful and complete. There was a favorite spot called Winkle Bar that had become so familiar that Grey knew he must have it for his own retreat. He bought the land and built a cottage large enough to accommodate the entire family, such guests as they would invite to share the fishing season, and all the fishing paraphernalia that was needed.

Wherever the whole family could gather together was home for Grey, but the place he called "permanent camp" was at Altadena, California. Here was a large, comfortable house with spacious rooms, quiet gardens, and shady trees. Here he and his family spent many happy days, enjoying their home life doubly because it meant reunion after long separation. It was the essence of all that home can mean to a man.

It was a far cry from the hall bedroom in New York where Zane Grey had embarked on his dubious career. Here was warmth and light and color. The clamor of traffic was supplanted by the singing of birds and the chattering of squirrels in the trees that encircled the house, and the view from the writer's study window was of the misty peak of Mt. Wilson instead of the towering framework of the elevated railway. He shuddered when he thought of the city. It was not his kind of life. When he was forced to go to New York on a business trip he hurried back gratefully to the peace and quiet and spaciousness of his western home.

It was a secluded place, half hidden from the road by a hedge of fir trees and surrounded on all sides by cool trees in which many kinds of birds nested and sang. A grassy lawn sloped away from the gravel driveway, and tall poplars lined the gravel footpath leading from the street. Through an archway was the path leading to the garden where Gray often worked, or simply sat beneath the trees inhaling the fragrance of the roses, orange blossoms, and magnolia. The garden was a riot of color in all seasons, for Grey was especially sensitive to color and fond of flowers of all kinds. Besides the rose garden —which was the only formal planting of the entire garden—there was a careless confusion of iris, sweet Williams, bachelor buttons, petunias, and African daisies, with a background of tall chrysanthemums, and poppies, green shrubbery, and trumpetvine. The mingled aromas of pine, cedar, and eucalyptus scented the air, permeating those rooms of the house that faced upon the garden. Cocos palms and bamboo trees lent an exotic touch to the landscape. Dry brown leaves gave the air a tangy, woodsy fragrance, and caused a pleasant rustling sound underfoot as he strolled through the garden. The gardener had been disturbed by Grey's instructions: "Never rake up leaves in my garden. Nature intended that leaves stay on the ground." But in time he learned that the fallen leaves added to the natural charm of the garden and he respected Mr. Grey's request.

The interior of the house was as comfortably casual as the garden and bespoke the remarkable genius of Dolly

Grey for homemaking, as well as her intuitive knowledge of the kind of atmosphere that gave her husband the greatest comfort and relaxation. In keeping with the Spanish style of architecture, with arched windows and doorways and wrought-iron balustrades, were colorful Navajo rugs and Mexican tapestries, pieces of Indian pottery and baskets, copper vases and bronze figurines, each with its background of personal history that doubled its intrinsic value.

The sunporch, with its comfortable chairs and convenient tables, commanded an excellent view of the terraced garden and, as an added attraction, always offered an inviting array of magazines. The living room was a homey place for family gatherings, with its woolly bearskin rugs, needlepoint chairs, a comfortable sofa, shelves of well-worn books, and convenient reading lamps. There was a red-brick fireplace on whose mantel stood Grey's favorite clipper-ship model, perfect in every detail. At one end of the room was a grand piano, and on it were family portraits in easel frames. The library beyond, with its light wicker furniture, was lined with books, the open shelves encircling the room to a height of six feet. Above the shelves were Indian wall paintings. On the floor were Navajo rugs, one a colorful Yebitchi rug purchased from an aged Indian in Arizona who said it was the only Navajo rug that had ever had twelve figures woven into it.

As time went by, the Greys found it necessary to build an addition to the original structure to house the curios and art objects that Grey had brought home from the far corners of the earth, as well as to give added space for "hobby equipment" and working room. The old wing was devoted entirely to living and sleeping quarters, allowing for ample and spacious bedrooms on the upper floor, while the new wing, added at right angles with the old and joined by an arched bridge, was reserved exclusively for writing, photography, hunting and fishing equipment, and all the accoutrements held dear to a sportsman's heart.

One could enter the new wing from the garden or through a door in the archway that led to the garden, or from a long hallway on the second floor that passed over the arch, making it secluded but easily accessible. The first floor of the new wing was divided into two rooms, one with rows of saddles and cupboards filled with trophies, souvenirs, and wildlife specimens from all over the world; the other with fishing rods and tackle of all descriptions. The walls of both rooms were covered with enlargements of photographs, mainly of fishing, all taken by Grey or his son, Romer. On the second floor was a room that might very well have been called the file room, for its walls were lined with built-in cupboards in which Grey kept great volumes of notes and "scribblings," pictures, books, trophies, and all sorts of mementoes that gave him inspiration. To offset the severity of the "file room" were more bright Indian blankets and rugs.

The writing den opened off the file room, on a slightly lower level to give it an air of greater privacy. The short flight of steps led down into a long, high-ceilinged room with dark oak cross-beams reinforced with wrought iron. Midway in the room were waist-high colonnades that gave the effect of dividing the room into two; on the shelves were Grey's favorite books, and on top were many personal treasures, mainly of Indian handicraft.

At one end of the room was a large picture window through which sunlight streamed, and a doorway leading to a private balcony that overlooked the garden. At the opposite end of the room was a huge fireplace which had been ornamented by R.C. with paintings of Indian symbols. The Indian motif was carried out on the home-spun drapes with simple appliques, the contribution of Dolly Grey.

There were other evidences of a woman's thoughtful touch in a room that was distinctly a man's room. There was, for example, the worn leather chair beside the fire-place. Since the days at Lackawaxen, when Grey's study was furnished with a table, a chair, and a wood stove, he had found that the best conditions for writing were a comfortable morris chair with a wide board stretched across from arm to arm, and a nearby table with a large supply of writing paper and sharp pencils. Wherever they lived, Mrs. Grey had always made sure that these essentials were present. In their various moves about the country, one of her first tasks in establishing a new home, or "pitching camp," as Grey preferred to call it, was visiting all the second-hand furniture stores in the neigh-borhood in search of a well-worn morris chair for the study. There was such a chair in all the "temporary camps"; the one in the "permanent camp" at Altadena was the same one in which he had sat while writing the first novel ever accepted by the House of Harper.

Often as he sat in the ancient chair by the fireplace, he reflected upon the amazing wisdom and understand-ing of his wife. Without her, he knew, he would still be struggling for the right channel of self-expression. It was she who had given moral support when none other—except, perhaps, R.C.—had faith in him. She knew instinctively all the conditions that contributed to his happiness and to his successful career. When he was im-mersed in his writing, she forbade interruptions, knowing that he was living the story as he wrote it and that any intrusion—even on her own part—would destroy the mood. How many times she had waited meals for him while he wrote on and on, forgetful of time and hunger! How many manuscripts she had read with him, suggesting, criticizing, encouraging! How many bothersome details of business she had handled in her own quiet, competent way, leaving him free to follow his creative pursuits!

She was like the pioneer wives of his Zane ancestors, demanding nothing, accepting him as he was. She understood perfectly that he must be free to roam about the world, hunting, fishing, exploring, always looking for new places and new material. She knew that for him variety was not the spice of life, but a basic need for existence, and if he were to write stories of adventure, he had to live a life of adventure. She never complained about his absences, nor did she attempt, in the manner of some of her modern contemporaries, to infringe upon the man's world in which he lived while he was away. There was no doubt that she missed him, and that he was always uppermost in her thoughts, but she had the companionship of the children, the diversified interests of homemaking, and innumerable business affairs to keep her occupied while he was away. He was doing his work; she had hers to do at home. And the fact that they both loved their work was the key to their accord.

Fishing in New Zealand Waters

The green forests of Oregon were a welcome change after months at sea, the early part of the year having been spent in the South Pacific and the summer months, as usual, at Avalon. As they fished for broadbill swordfish off the Catalina coast, Grey and R.C. often spoke of the Rogue River and their plans to follow it from its headwaters through the Cascade Range to the point where it flowed into the Pacific at Gold Beach.

When the time came to leave Avalon, however, R.C. could not tear himself away from the pursuit of swordfish, so Grey set out for Grants Pass with Romer and Captain Mitchell, who had never before seen the Northwest and was charmed by its scenic wonders. The indispensable Takahashi was with them, and the drivers, Ken and Ed, completed the party. At Grants Pass they were met by their guide, Bardon, who had spent most of his life there as a market fisherman, and his young helper, Van Dorn. "Lone Angler" Wiborn and his wife, with other Oregon friends and fishermen, were on hand to see the party embark on their daring trek down river through regions that were little known except to lum-

171

bermen and native fishermen. There were many warnings as to the dangers to be encountered, and Grey smiled inwardly as he recalled the Santa Rosa adventure and the well-meant admonitions that preceded it.

He was reminded of that jungle expedition many times in the days that followed, whenever he heard the ominous roar of rapids ahead and felt the sickening sensation of catastrophe as the rushing waters lashed his boat uncomfortably near the rocks. On this expedition, however, there were six boats, all carefully constructed especially for the journey, and the loss of one, though it might entail the loss of good equipment, would not necessarily spell doom for its occupants, as would surely have been the case had he and Pepe and George Allen been stranded in the Tamaulipas jungle without means of transportation.

At the end of the first day, Grey chalked up the score: ten miles covered, seventeen rapids, two leaky boats and one lost on the way. His own boat had struck a rock and sprung a leak, but it was balm to his ego, though a disappointing loss, when the boat piloted by Bardon, the expert guide and boatman, suffered worse damage. The cargo was saved and distributed among the other five boats, which meant that they were all loaded too heavily for best balance. Grey vowed that in future he would restrict his equipment to a bare minimum.

They were fortunate in finding an excellent campsite where three picturesque streams with striking names—Rum Creek, Whiskey Creek, and Booze Creek—flowed into the Rogue within a half mile's distance. These creeks had been named by lusty prospectors who had been the first men to enter the Rogue Valley. There were a few gold mines still being worked in the vicinity, one by a lone prospector who had lived there in the hills for ten years. He visited the Grey camp, brought gifts of venison for Takahashi to cook, and invited the men to come up to his garden and shoot the deer that trampled recklessly through it.

Grey did decide to stay on for a few days, not for the purpose of accepting the invitation, but partly because the men wanted to try their luck at salmon fishing and partly because Bardon had offered to walk back to the abandoned boat and see if it could be salvaged. While he and his assistant accomplished that task successfully, the others devoted themselves, without notable success, to the pleasures of fishing. There had been heavy rains which left the river muddy and swollen, and there were no signs of a run of steelhead such as Grey and R.C. had witnessed the preceding year. But the scenery was restful, Takahashi's food enjoyable, and there were countless little forest creatures to draw the interest of a nature-lover.

In a talk with the old prospector, Grey learned that the Forest Service was planning to cut a military road through this section. The prospector was violently opposed to it, and Grey shared his feeling, for although he realized that the intent back of the plan was worthy, he had seen, especially in California, the harm that was done when virgin timberland was opened to automobile traffic. These roads invariably led to the increase, rather than decrease, of forest fires and in addition placed a heavy toll on the wild life of the forest when easy accessibility encouraged the invasion of city hunters and fishermen. Grey felt a twinge of regret with the thought that the America he knew was vanishing. He was glad that enough of it remained for Romer to see it as he had in his own boyhood; but for Romer's sons he feared these adventures would never be experienced.

Romer was making the most of it, as if he were keenly aware of his precious heritage and the brevity of time allotted him to enjoy it. He lived each day to the fullest, with a zest and vigor that amazed members of the party who had not seen him for a year. To Grey himself the change in Romer was not so obvious, for it had been accomplished gradually as he watched the lad from day to day, but now and again a striking incident would remind him that his son was practically a grown man. During those days on the Rogue River, he frequently outstripped his father, who was admittedly weary from the year's heavy schedule and possibly weakened somewhat by a tonsillectomy he had undergone that summer.

Grey would have been happy to remain encamped at Whiskey Creek for a while longer, but as soon as the damaged boat was afloat again, they broke camp and said goodbye to their prospector friend, who came down to the river to see them off and wish them luck in fervent tones which indicated his unexpressed belief that they would need it.

In the second day of shooting rapids, Romer became more daring than ever and more than a little indignant when his father forbade him to risk what appeared to be a particularly treacherous chute. His temper flared briefly as he declared he could do it with one hand tied behind him. His confidence was not shared by George Takahashi, his sole passenger, who promptly deserted him when Grey reluctantly gave his consent. The time had come for Romer to assert his manhood; it was not fair to delay it in favor of a father's fears. So with his heart frozen within him, Grey stood on an overhanging cliff and watched the boy shove off into the swift current, grapple with the choppy waves, and strike a half-submerged rock with a glancing blow that shot the boat up into the air. Grey was paralyzed with a fear he had never known when his own safety was at stake, but Romer, calm and self-assured, never lost his grip on the oars. The boat dropped back into the channel in upright position and Romer kept it that way to the foot of the rapids.

The boy was as quick to belittle his achievement as he was to tease his father when the latter had trouble handling his own craft in treacherous rapids. "Say, dad," Romer would shout, "how did you ever manage the Santa Rosa?" And Grey wondered himself at the change a decade could produce in a man's personality. He had now reached the half-century mark and although the years had not marked him with age they had taught him things that made him regard many of his past performances as acts of foolhardy youth. No longer was he willing to take needless risks, particularly where the lives of others were involved. He had not forgotten the dark night on the bow of the *Fisherman* when his conscience had flayed him for leading his friends, his brother, and his son to the brink of disaster.

Despite Grey's firm resolve to exercise caution throughout the Rogue River journey, there were times when the unforeseeable happened, as on the occasion when his boat and Captain Mitchell's accidentally became locked together and were swept into a current that would have been perilous enough for one boat alone. Somehow, without knowing how it was done, Grey managed to disengage the locked boats in time to avert the catastrophe that appeared certain, and when both boats were safely beached he was confronted by a white-faced Romer who glared at him and demanded almost belligerently, "What were you trying to do—scare me to death?"

On the long homestretch, after many days of rowing and many more days of fishing, Grey proved his endurance was as strong as ever and won his son's greatest tribute. Everyone was tired, and even Romer had lost his zest and energy, to say nothing of his good disposition. He grumbled about his sore muscles and blistered hands, he was bored with the scenery, he was hungry and he was tired of rowing. Watching the signs of fatigue develop, Grey was a bit relieved at these proofs that Romer, though quite grown-up in many respects, was still only a boy. His own example of good humor and patient, steady rowing were not wasted on the boy, for he suddenly remarked: "Dad, I've always noticed how you get a second wind—or spirit—or something—and keep on going at the last when everybody else has quit or is half dead."

It was the finest compliment Romer had ever paid him, and Grey was glad he had made no complaints about his own sore hands and aching back. He was as weary as anyone else, but he was a hero in the eyes of his son, so what did it matter?

In that moment of exultation he heard the welcome roar in the distance—the rhythmic beating of the Pacific on the sands of Gold Beach.

Another dream had been realized—and yet another was rapidly taking the form of a concrete plan. For in the evenings around the campfire, Grey and Captain Mitchell had talked at great length of exploring further the fishing grounds of the South Seas. Even as they fished for salmon and steelhead, they were speaking of swordfish and tuna.

Back at Altadena, detailed plans were formulated and preparations were made. R.C. could not leave at that time and Romer needed to concentrate on his studies, so Grey and Mitchell resolved to make it a two-man expedition rather than postpone it longer. Accordingly, the last day of that year found them outward bound aboard the Royal Mail S.S. *Makura*, heading southwest for the Antipodes, while the *Fisherman* lay at anchor in San Francisco Bay.

Shipboard acquaintances are quickly made and Captain Mitchell soon found friends in the Radmore brothers who had been reared in the same part of England in which he had been born and who, like himself, had served in World War I. They had traveled all over the world, had hunted and fished on every continent, and had many interesting tales to tell of big game hunts in Africa, Burma, and India; of pearl-fishing off the coast of New Guinea, where an innocent native once traded a $16,000 pearl for a can of peaches. The Radmores had been to New Zealand several times but could give no information as to the fishing possibilities in the surrounding waters, thus giving Grey the happy impression that he was heading for virgin seas, as far as fishing was concerned.

Grey was frankly shocked by Papeete, the renowned French port in Tahiti which was their first stop on the voyage. Although he had read much about it, and had been particularly impressed by *White Shadows of the South Seas*, he had not anticipated the degeneracy he saw all about him on his one day ashore. "I did not wonder," he wrote, "that Robert Louis Stevenson went to the South Seas a romancer and became a militant moralist." Liquor was almost as cheap as water and appeared to be twice as abundant. All through the day hotels and bars were crowded with coarse drunken men and women of loose morals. The white men who lived there appeared pale and sickly to Grey, and he reiterated his conviction that "the Creator did not intend white

men to live on South Sea Islands; if he had he would
have made the pigment of their skins capable of resist-
ing the sun."

The natives were far more interesting than the whites.
Little brown children, innocent of clothing, played happily on the beach. In sharp contrast there were old men
who, Grey was certain, must in their time have fed
upon human flesh, called "long pig." "The record seemed
written in their great strange eyes," he said.

Most welcome surprise was the sight of the Tahitian
women, so often portrayed as the voluptuous dancing-
girl type. Grey, who had clung to his ideals of masculine
chivalry and feminine refinement, had been revolted by
the advent of the "Flapper Age" in America, so marked
when, on his return from the first Pacific cruise, he
walked down city streets or strolled along the beach at
Avalon. Like all lovers of natural beauty, he abhorred
anything gaudy or artificial, and in reply to those who
shrugged their shoulders and said, "Times change," he
was wont to say, "Not always for the better." Feeling as
he did about the difference time had wrought in civilized
woman, it was natural for him to record his personal
reactions to the native women of Papeete:

"The Tahitian women presented an agreeable surprise
to me. From all the exotic photographs I had seen I had
not been favorably impressed. But photographs do not
do justice to Tahitian women. I saw hundreds of them,
and except in a few cases, noticeably the dancers, who
in fact were faked to impress the tourists, they were
modestly dressed and graceful in appearance. They were
strong, well built though not voluptuous, rather light
skinned. . . . [with] large melting melancholy eyes.
They wore their hair in braids down their backs, like
American schoolgirls of long ago when something of

178

America still survived in our girls. These Tahitians had light brown, sometimes nut-brown and chestnut hair, rich and thick and beautiful. What a delight to see! What pleasure to walk behind one of these barefooted and free-stepping maidens just for the innocent happiness of gazing at her wonderful braid! No scrawny shaved bristled necks, such as the flappers exhibit now, to man's bewildered disgust; no erotic and abnormal signs of wanting to resemble a male! Goodness only knows why so-called civilized white women of modern times want to look like men, but so it seems they do. If they could see the backs of the heads of these Tahitian girls and their long graceful braids of hair, that even a fool of a man could tell made very little trouble, and was so exquisitely feminine and beautiful, they might have a moment of illumined mind."

Papeete was sticky with humid heat, and after the day ashore it was good to be underway again, heading into the cool sea breeze. Three more days brought the *Makura* to the British-controlled island of Roratonga, where passengers were again permitted to go ashore. Here was a scene far more in keeping with the white man's dream of a South Seas paradise. Village streets were clean and quiet in contrast to the noisy drunken brawling on the streets of Papeete. Grey learned that liquor was banned on the island, which accounted for a great deal, although the natives were of a different race, carefree and contented, with none of the brooding appearance of the sad-eyed Tahitians.

Grey and his companions, Captain Mitchell and the Radmores, found that the drowsy charm of the island cast a spell upon them, and although they were all interested in spending some time there later in quest of the giant swordfish reputed to be plentiful in nearby waters, Grey concluded that it might be risky to linger there very long. Surely the enchantment of the atmosphere could induce forgetfulness of civilization and even the happiest of homes.

Leaving Roratonga, the *Makura* crossed the International Date Line, thereby skipping a date on the calendar, and on the following day Grey caught his first "absolutely certain sight" of an albatross. On a few occasions he thought he had glimpsed them from the deck of the *Fisherman*, but no one had been able to identify them positively from that distance, which had been something of a disappointment to Grey, for he loved birds and had always been singularly intrigued by the phantom albatross in the *Rime of the Ancient Mariner*. He was not disappointed in the actual vision, for the bird followed the wake of the *Makura* for miles, sailing with graceful ease all alone in the sky.

There were more albatrosses to be seen as the *Makura* approached New Zealand, but even more exciting was the appearance of a broadbill swordfish of amazing size, only fifteen miles offshore. New Zealand promised to be all that a fisherman could wish.

From Wellington, the point of debarkation, Grey and Mitchell proceeded by rail to Auckland and thence to the village of Russell where fishing boats were awaiting them, according to prearrangement. Grey was surprised to learn how his fame had spread abroad, for small boys of the village having heard of his coming, gathered around to greet him. They had read the English editions of many of his books, which were obtainable at all New Zealand bookstores, and were intent upon meeting the author. Disappointment registered on their faces for reasons that Grey could not understand until one of the youngsters confessed that they had expected to see him wearing chaps, spurs, cowboy boots, ten-gallon hat, and a gun at each hip. The girls, on the other hand, were disappointed on discovering that the author of the Zane Grey romances was not a woman! This impression was so common that Grey mused briefly on the futility of changing his given name.

Among local fishermen his name and reputation as an angler were well known, for he had corresponded for many years with anglers all over the world, concentrating more recently on those of New Zealand in order to gain information on fishing prospects, bait and tackle and methods used. At the hotel he engaged in many discussions with men who were interested in deep-sea fishing, a sport which was in its infancy in New Zealand at that time, as evidenced by the crude equipment available. Grey and Mitchell, learning that even this poor tackle had landed two-hundred-pound tuna, were eager to see what could be accomplished with their own specially-designed equipment.

They started their fishing expedition as soon as weather allowed, working from a small privately-owned island off the coast, where they had pitched their tents on a green slope shaded by fragrant, lacy "ti" trees and frequented by myriads of birds with melodious songs. Because of these, Grey gave this temporary home the name "Camp of the Larks." The English sportsman, Alma Baker, joined them later, and the Radmores dropped in occasionally. Other members of the party were two cameramen from the States and the four boatmen picked up in Russell, all of whom had seen active duty in the World War and could tell hair-raising stories of their experiences. One of Mitchell's men aroused all of Grey's wartime bitterness with his narrative of the German torpedo that had sunk the clearly-marked hospital ship on which he, and hundreds of other wounded soldiers, were being transported home. He was one of the handful that were saved.

These hardy boatmen were outgrowing the effects of the war under the healing influence of the clean outdoor life at sea, and it was a pleasure to Grey to see their enthusiasm for their work and the keen admiration they expressed for the magnificent fishing gear he and Mitchell had brought with them. Never had they seen anything like it.

Their excitement knew no bounds when Grey landed the first broadbill swordfish ever to be caught on a rod in New Zealand waters, and followed up this achievement by chalking up new records, one after the other: the world's record catch for one day, ten fish averaging more than 250 pounds each; world record striped marlin, 450 pounds; a black marlin weighing 704 pounds; world record yellowtail, 111 pounds. Captain Mitchell, with his 976-pound black marlin, set a world record for all species of fish ever caught with rod and line, so large that it had to be cut in three pieces to be weighed. As usual, the greatest excitement of all was over the fish that got away, the fish in this case being a mako, considered by New Zealanders to be the mightiest fighter in those waters and among the largest species, for they frequently were seen to measure twenty feet long and weigh more than a ton. Captain Mitchell hooked one that must have weighed at least twelve hundred pounds, but no one could ever verify the estimate for as he reeled in the vicious fighter, it lunged into the air in one last desperate defense and broke away. The only consolation surviving the loss was the beautiful photograph caught in the last round of the battle.

Grey's main regret was not over the many fish they

had lost but over the fact that Romer and R.C. had not been present to share the adventure. As they prepared to break Camp of the Larks, he silently vowed he would return, bringing his son and brother with him. Before that time came he knew the two of them would devour his carefully kept journal on the happenings of this expedition, the flora and fauna of New Zealand, and the strange new varieties of fish he had encountered.

Grey could not have left New Zealand without exploring the mainland and trying his luck at fresh-water fishing in the inland lakes and rivers. During the inland journey he delighted in photographing the scenic wonders of New Zealand, the most striking of which was the Waitomo glowworm cave, a limestone formation through which a subterranean river flowed while overhead shone millions of tiny blue lights where glowworms clung to the roof of the cave.

He spent some time with the Maori tribes and learned much of their folklore and legend. He had always thought of the Maoris as an uncivilized tribe, so he was surprised to find them a cultured and educated people. One night he attended a Maori concert and was startled to hear the master of ceremonies say in flawless English: "Greetings and salutations to Zane Grey, who has come from far to conquer the leviathans of the deep. We wish to bestow upon him the name of Maui, after our Maui legend of the great fisherman of the Maoris." Grey was embarrassed to discover that he was well known among these people, of whose culture he had hitherto been unaware. Many of them had read his books; he saw the tattered volumes everywhere.

There were further evidences of the writer's widespread popularity. He was touched by the deluge of letters he received from school children all over New

Zealand. One of them enclosed a poem to him titled "My Favorite Author." The honors bestowed on him in this faraway land impressed him with "the appalling responsibility of a novelist who in these modern days of materialism dares to foster idealism and love of nature, chivalry in men and chastity in women."

Not all the public notice Grey received was wholly complimentary. One elderly gentleman, disgusted with newspaper accounts of the Zane Grey expedition, wrote: "See here, all this fuss about your coming 7000 miles with high-priced newfangled machinery to catch swordfish is sort of ridiculous. Sonny, I caught New Zealand swordfish before you were born, and did it with hairpins, too." The irate correspondent was doubtless referring to the small gar-fish which grew only a few inches long and because of its spear-like nose was erroneously called swordfish by youthful anglers.

For many days, Zane Grey engaged in a controversy, via the columns of a local newspaper, regarding the use of the triple (or gang) hook in New Zealand. It was his contention that the use of such a murderous hook robs the fish of a sporting chance, and he stated in no uncertain terms that a ten-year-old child should be able to catch a swordfish on such a hook. In his opinion, it was unsportsmanlike; he insisted on using a single hook and waging a fair battle. Many anglers, like the old man who had caught swordfish with a hairpin, were opposed to his "newfangled gear" and resented his comments, while others saw his point and changed their tactics. It could not be said that either side actually won the debate; but the discussion undoubtedly provided inspiration for organizing a sporting club in New Zealand for fishing and hunting.

In a lighter vein, an Auckland newspaper carried the

story of two old gentlemen who had read of Zane Grey's visit to New Zealand while he was staying at Russell.

"It says," one of them read, "that he came to absorb local color. What do you reckon that might be?"

"That's easy!" the other scoffed. "He's gettin' himself sunburnt. I've been to Russell and *I know*!"

One of the greatest surprises of his New Zealand sojourn occurred off Cape Brett, when Grey's boat met an old fishing sloop with the name *Desert Gold* on her stern. The coincidence was peculiarly striking because that was the title of the book which had been the basis for his meeting with Sievert Nielsen. Inquiries proved that it was not mere coincidence; the market fisherman who owned the boat assured him that it was, indeed, named for the Zane Grey novel. He volunteered the further information that the title had also provided the name for one of the greatest race horses ever bred in the Antipodes.

Small wonder it was that Grey, as he boarded the *Makura's* sister ship, the S.S. *Tahiti*, for the return voyage, felt that he was saying farewell to his second home. Eagerly he anticipated the day when he could return. Romer would be wild about New Zealand.

Father and Son

The passing years did not dull Zane Grey's craving for new adventures and distant lands. He was always convinced—and experience repeatedly bore it out—that the next camp would be even more beautiful than the last, and that the adventures of the past were as nothing compared to those of the future. Yet paradoxically each new journey increased his anticipation of homecoming. Sometimes, in his eagerness to speed the day of reunion with his family, he wondered why he ever left home at all.

This question was often in his mind in the restless days at sea while the *Tahiti* made her leisurely progress from New Zealand to San Francisco. There was an irritating sense of standing helpless while time rushed by. Home had never before looked so good to a wanderer, and Grey felt a shock as he realized how quickly the children were growing up. Even a few months made a world of difference. Romer was very manly in voice and bearing, with an insatiable hunger for the outdoors and all the knowledge that pertained to it. Betty was in her teens and acting more like a young lady than a tomboy schoolgirl. She was quiet and studious, loved to read and write poetry, and had already produced some very promising verse.

The greatest change was in Loren, the youngest of the three, now the age that Romer had been when he went on his first hunting trip into the Tonto Basin. To Grey, it was incredible and appalling that Loren, who had been but a baby when that trip was planned, was now of an age to carry a rifle himself and have his own fishing rods. Yet it seemed only a few weeks ago that Romer was gaining his introduction to outdoor living. With a pang of regret, he thought how quickly Romer had grown to manhood in the brief years after their first hunt together, and he resolved to enjoy Loren's boyhood to the fullest.

He was constantly amazed at the little lad, who was so unlike the older brother. Loren, too, was fond of the outdoors, but in a very different way, for he was quiet and dreamy, with a totally unconscious faculty for provoking laughter. Now and again he roused from his reveries to perform feats that surprised everyone, then promptly lapsed back into his private dreamland, in a way that reminded one of Stevenson's remark that "The thoughts of youth are long, long thoughts."

In the summer after Grey's joyous return from New Zealand, while he was at Avalon for the fishing season, Loren was attending the boys' camp on Catalina Island, and there distinguished himself by winning the camp award for fishing. Besides the prize, he won the title of "Big Fish," spontaneously bestowed on him by his admiring fellows, and, what was much more precious to him, permission to accompany his father on the autumn trip to Rogue River.

That year Grey bought Winkle Bar from an old prospector who held the mining claim on it, and there the party camped while they fished the Rogue for steelhead. It was a record year for everyone except Takahashi and Grey. Romer and Captain Mitchell were neck and neck for top honors, and R.C. was not far behind. The drivers, Ken and Ed, who were becoming indispensable to any Z.G. expedition, found their luck had improved vastly since their first acquaintance with Rogue River fishing. Takahashi summed up his fishing experiences in the unabashed report: "All same like last year! Hook steelhead, he jump high, then run under rock and stick there!"

As for Grey, he was willing to admit that it was an off-season for him and was no more perturbed at the admission than was the luckless Takahashi. In ten days of fishing he had caught only three steelheads, compared with Romer's thirty, but he had never had a more enjoyable experience. He was content to loaf in the shade and rest his sea-weary eyes on the green-wooded Oregon landscape, to listen to the sweet music of the birds and the singing river, and to enjoy the companionship of his two sons and his brother. He spent hours observing Loren and instructing him in angling and nature lore. The boy acquitted himself so well on the expedition that Grey, who had entertained some misgivings about bringing him, resolved to make the Winkle Bar expedition the following year a family affair, adding his wife and daughter to the party. He did not want his family to grow away from him, and whenever it could be arranged for them to share his adventures it was so much the better.

As far as the quest for new material was concerned, Grey became increasingly aware that he had been seeking it too far afield, overlooking a wealth of ideas and inspiration in his own family and home. A day with

Loren, for example, provided an amazing series of reactions—wonder, nostalgia, pathos, and laughter—and from these observations he wrote the most revealingly human article of his entire career. It was a word-portrait so skillful that it could have been painted only by a very proud and discerning father.

"I never saw a lad like him," Grey wrote. "He was hardly a boy. He was an elf, a spirit. He spent hours watching lizards, bugs, worms—and if he could get a live trout in a little corral of rocks he was wholly content. He was not afraid to pick up anything. As for poison oak, which ran rampant, he would vigorously rub his hands with the treacherous leaves and exclaim, 'Never touches me—that poison oak!' . . . As for snakes —they were his favorite dish. Many times I caught him tearing up the rocks in pursuit. It did no good to command him to leave the snakes alone, or read him a severe lecture upon possible danger. Straightway he forgot both. The only solution was to watch him, and this indeed was next to impossible. He ran here, there, everywhere. He flitted about the camp like the little Oregon junco. . . .

"Gophers and ground squirrels held irresistible fascination for Loren. Like a dog he would dig for them. He never caught any, but that made no difference. He was indefatigable in pursuit. He manifested the destructive boy's instinct in regard to the snakes and lizards, but I did not discover that he wanted to kill anything else."

There were countless indelible pictures to store away in the father's memory: of Loren returning to camp with a string of fish, with dripping sodden clothing and the stench of fish all about him, with his fishing rod broken and his eyes tragic over the big fish that broke the rod and got away; of Loren listening with impish smile while his father delivered a lecture on the care of fishing tackle; of Loren with his new fishing-rod, poking it down into a gopher-hole to rout its frightened tenant; of Loren crying pathetically over a lost fly, or beaming radiantly over a fifteen-inch steelhead.

Of the vivid episodes that made this excursion a particularly fond memory for Grey, perhaps the most outstanding was the tragicomic incident of Loren and his fishpond. While the others were fishing, the boy gathered up rocks from along the river bank and at the edge of the stream carefully constructed a circular wall, thus forming a little artificial pond of his own. This was intended for the fish he never seemed to be able to catch. R.C. took pity on the luckless young angler and, after hooking a small steelhead on his own rod, turned it over to the boy. Loren was proud as a peacock at being trusted with his uncle's rod, and even prouder when he landed the fish. Gently he removed the hook and hurried off to put his catch in the fishpond. When darkness fell upon the camp, Grey went out to look for his younger son and at the riverbank came upon a scene that is best described in his own words:

"Lorry was sitting on a stone beside his pond, his elbows on his knees and his hands covering his face. His posture was one of extreme dejection. R.C. was standing, rod in hand, looking down at the boy.

" 'Lorry, what's the matter?' I inquired.

"The lad flung up his hands dramatically. 'Oh, my God! Oh, my God!' he cried.

" 'Son, I don't see any occasion for such talk,' I returned, reprovingly.

" 'My trout jumped out of the pond. He got away,' replied Loren, tragically.

190

" 'Too bad. But you'll get another tomorrow. Come, it's late. Let's go to camp,' I said consolingly.

" 'Don't mind, Lorry,' added my brother. 'If you're going to be a fisherman you must learn early that all the big ones get away.'

"We climbed the gravel bar and entered the oak grove, where it was quite dark. Here Loren slipped his little cold wet hand in mine and trudged to camp in eloquent silence. Just before we reached the camp fire he whispered: 'Dad, don't tell Romer about me losing the trout. He'd make fun of me.' "

Loren as an angler aroused all of Grey's sympathy, for he himself had always claimed to be a "hard-luck" fisherman, except for rare flashes of good fortune. It seemed that Loren was destined to follow in his footsteps, for though he was patient and was becoming more skilled at casting, his record was not remarkable on this first expedition, and even less so the following year when the entire family came to Winkle Bar.

It was a grand occasion for the Greys. It was the first time they had all been in camp together. Only R.C. was missing; he had hit a lucky streak in swordfishing at Avalon and was afraid to break the spell. Nothing could have induced Grey, however, to forego the Rogue River trip, for seven months in New Zealand and among the South Sea Islands—accompanied this time by Romer— had made him eager for a change of scenery. Moreover, he had made extensive plans for taking the family to Oregon and he was determined not to let anything stand in the way of their vacation.

According to plan, the party included Captain Mitchell, Ken and Ed, and Takahashi, besides members of the family. Then at the last minute Romer asked permission to bring three of his friends, whereupon Loren claimed the right to invite one guest for himself. Boy-like, he was intent upon displaying to his friend Gus his own prowess as a fisherman, but as usual, fortune forsook him in favor of Gus; it was Gus who brought in the fifteen-inch steelhead, while Loren fished for days without a single catch. To make matters more humiliating, even his sister Betty caught a two-pound trout.

Even the best of equipment did not help. Grey took this occasion to present Loren with a fine new fishing rod. First the boy snagged the new tapered line and lost it; then he broke the tip of his rod, replaced it and broke a second tip; then he spent hours repairing it. At last, to his father's mingled disapproval and amusement, he resorted to grasshopper bait, defending his sportsmanship by announcing that even President Coolidge fished for trout with worms.

"That's quite true," Grey admitted, "but a lot of high-brow fly fishermen criticized him for it. Not that I agree with them," he went on, "for there are times and places where you have to use bait if you're going to catch any fish. But here in the Rogue I've never found it necessary, and I'd like for you to get some practice at fly-casting while you're here."

Loren wasn't enthusiastic on the subject. He had spent six days of fly-casting, with no striking results except to snag himself in the seat of the pants and suffer the added discomfiture of finding people laughing at him. His father decided that Loren could stand a day of close supervision if he were to improve his technique and outgrow his angler's complex, so the two set out together for a day on the river. As it turned out, it was a case of the halt leading the blind, for Grey's luck was worse than usual and he was unable even to hook a fish to be turned over to Loren for the final catch. By the end of the day, Grey had given up in exhaustion, but Loren fished on—again with grasshoppers as bait, toward sundown. Still he caught nothing, and Grey feared that Loren would not only lose interest in fishing but lose respect for his father's angling ability as well. But Loren proved that he had caught the true outdoor spirit from his father when, as they trudged wearily back toward camp, he concluded that "you don't have to catch fish to have a good day."

A Wanderer Comes Home

Zane Grey was a family man at heart, and he made the most of the time he spent with his wife and children. They played tennis together, fished, went horseback riding, and occasionally he and Dolly Grey took time out for a motor trip along the beautiful California coast or through the redwood forests, although Grey was outspokenly antagonistic toward "noisy, stinking automobiles" and far preferred to see the beauties of nature from the back of a horse. They had their gatherings at the Tonto Basin lodge at Avalon and at Winkle Bar. But Grey's restless spirit and inquisitive mind always led him to far fields, filling his life with adventure and infinite variety.

A typical year in the life of Zane Grey would include, besides the writing of two novels and several articles, a deep-sea fishing expedition in Pacific waters, the spring months at Altadena, the summer at Avalon, a trip into the desert to act as adviser to a movie company on location filming one of his books, hunting in Arizona or fishing in Oregon, a much-dreaded business trip to New York, topped off with a fishing expedition at Long Key, where he was for many years president of the Fishing Club. During his travels he kept his eyes open for changes in the American scene and possible settings for his romances, for to him setting was more important than story. He never consciously sought local color; rather, he was deeply interested in places, and when he found a scene that made a particular impression on him, his active imagination would automatically begin weaving a story against that background.

So it was with Boulder City, in the days of the construction of the great dam. Grey was vastly interested in this project to control the Colorado River for man's purposes, and from his own memory of the formidable terrain of that area he imagined the undertaking to be well-nigh impossible. To satisfy his curiosity, he had to see for himself. After lengthy correspondence, he arranged with the contractors to visit the site and observe the inner workings of the project.

Arriving at Las Vegas, Nevada, he was amazed at the change in the sleepy western village he had visited some years before. He found it a busy humming city with automobiles lined up in parking places at the curb and people swarming the shops and sidewalks. It was a boom town, and as such, it had attracted much of the bad element: the gamblers, the grafters, dishonest professional men and unscrupulous merchants. There were dingy saloons, gambling dens, noisy dance halls, and rows of brothels. He met the chief of police, a Texas Ranger imported by the law-abiding citizens of Las Vegas to make war on the criminal underworld, and learned to his surprise that even in this dangerous environment the Ranger went unarmed, enforcing the law with his fists, if necessary, in preference to gunplay.

At Boulder City, law and order of the highest type prevailed under government control. Grey was impressed by the efficiency of the management, and the courtesy extended to him by the Six Companies, who had provided a competent guide to show him about the city. He had traveled over every inch of this territory by horseback in the Twenties, and now he was amazed to find a neatly laid-out little town with housing for the three thousand families employed at the site, paved streets, modern shops, motion picture theatres, athletic grounds, libraries and recreational facilities. There was a large restaurant, impeccably clean and capable of handling fifteen hundred men at a time.

In sharp contrast to the quiet, orderly little city was the dam site itself, only six miles distant. There quiet was unknown. Trucks, cars, steam shovels, air guns and men milling about by the thousands all added to the constant din. He was especially fascinated by the scalers and drillers, hanging from long ropes attached to the tops of the cliffs, swinging over the precipitous walls six or seven hundred feet high, apparently oblivious of the swift and horrible death that would claim them at the slightest accident.

Grey walked through the dam, where the concrete had already been poured to a height of 250 feet, and into the diversion tunnels that were not then in use, where he witnessed the operations of the hard-rock miners chiseling through the solid rocks with air guns and dynamite. Then he climbed the stairway leading up the side of the perpendicular cliff to look down upon the location of the power house where the turbines would eventually manufacture electricity that would provide electric energy for the people within a radius of a thousand miles. He observed the cement plant, the rock crusher, the concrete mixing mill, the miles of road and railroad track and bridges that had been constructed before this gigantic task could be launched.

Standing on a high observation point at dusk, he was amazed at the sudden miraculous transformation when the whole scene was illumined by thousands of flood-lights, making the entire area as bright as by daylight and enabling the men to continue work through the night. With four shifts, twenty-four hours a day, the project was rapidly advancing. Once again Grey found himself tremendously impressed by the battle between man and the elements, with man in this case coming through with flying colors.

The whole experience was so thrilling to him that he could not get it out of his mind, and as he thought it over and recalled all the details of the dam project and the fascinating life in the neighboring boom town, he began to conceive a story based on this background. He had gone to Boulder City only to satisfy his own curiosity; by the time he returned, he was well on the way to formulating the plot for *Code of the West*. Thus it was that most of his novels came into being.

With his keen powers of observation, Zane Grey had probably seen more of the United States than any man of his time, yet there was always much more to be seen than time would allow. He wanted to see other parts of the world, too. He had visited Havana and Rio, had spent much time in Mexico and Yucatan, had journeyed into Canada and fished off the coasts of Nova Scotia and Vancouver. He had made good his promise to himself to return to New Zealand, which he did a number of times, the voyage in the spring of 1928 being particu-

larly enjoyable for he was accompanied by Romer and
R.C. On their return trip, they had stopped off at Tahiti,
where the *Fisherman* was awaiting them. This was Zane
Grey's fourth visit to Papeete, but it was his most pleasant one, for his son and brother were seeing it for the
first time. Captain Mitchell was a member of the party,
and Romer's friend Johnny Shields was also included.
Everyone was so enthusiastic over fishing in these tropic
waters that they agreed to return the following year,
which they did, camping again at the familiar Flower
Point site. On this trip, Romer brought another friend,
young Bob Carney, who was destined later to marry
Betty Grey.

Tahitian waters yielded many new and strange species
of fish, the most interesting to Grey being marlin. He
caught one which he named the silver marlin, the first
of its kind to be caught, unless perhaps by native fishermen, and on a later expedition, in 1930, he landed a 1200-
pound monster which he named the giant Tahitian
striped marlin. He received countless radio messages of
congratulations on this amazing feat, including one from
Dolly Grey which read: "What ho, Ulysses! You've
hooked a better fish at home, which *might* get away." It
was signed "Penelope."

Grey appreciated the humor of his wife's jests, but
often asked himself seriously why Ulysses ever left home.
He had intentions of settling down some day. But there
were many new lands to explore, and it was typical of
Grey that he had to go and see for himself.

He had long been interested in Australia—an interest
which was mutual, for his books were widely read in
that country, as evidenced by the bewildering number
of letters he received from his Australian readers. One,

which proved his fame at home as well as abroad, was a letter addressed simply:

> Zane Grey, Esq.
> Big Game Fisherman and Novelist
> U.S.A.

It was delivered to him at his home in Altadena in record time.

It was not until 1936 that he finally made his long-planned voyage to Australia, after carrying on extensive correspondence with missionaries, merchant fishermen, sportsmen, naturalists, and business men with regard to the country's physical aspects, the fishing prospects, equipment used and the possibilities of outfitting locally. He spent many months in preparation, even to the point of ordering a launch specially built to his specifications at Auckland. From this launch, the *Avalon*, he hoped to catch some of the monstrous fish his correspondents had mentioned.

Arriving in Sydney on New Year's Eve, Grey was in time to enter the informal competition for "the first catch of 1936." His party—including his manager, Ed Bowen, and two cameramen—camped near the village of Bermagui, 275 miles down the coast from Sydney, and Grey forgot all the wearisome, nerve-wracking weeks of preparation for the expedition when he succeeded in bringing in the first marlin of 1936. Besides this distinction, he established an Australian record for both black marlin and striped marlin, his catches weighing 480 and 324 pounds, respectively, and as a climax to the Australian adventure, brought in a world-record tiger shark weighing 1036 pounds.

It was a fishing experience such as he had never had before. He learned that the Australians shot sharks, and justifiably so, for they were maneaters, and to kill one might mean the saving of a life. Among American anglers, such a practice might have been considered unsportsmanlike, but as Grey pointed out, the shark menace in Australia is far too great to be considered mere sport; it boils down to a matter of life and death. His own world-record tiger shark was gaffed rather than shot as he hauled it up to the boat, but his thrill in the catch came not so much from the sport as from the realization that those murderous fangs would never mutilate a human being.

It was supposed to be a poor season that year, but Grey's party caught 67 large fish weighing nearly ten tons, within four months, at least half of which were beached because of bad weather and high winds. Ed Bowen caught an 800-pound tiger shark, and Grey caught a "white-death" shark somewhat larger. On one occasion, he caught a whaler shark weighing 890 pounds and measuring twelve feet long, too large to be hauled aboard. In the end, they were forced to fasten it to the stern of the boat with heavy ropes and tow it fifteen miles to shore. There were gray nurse sharks, "sleek, shiny, lean and wolfish," in these waters. Grey caught six of them in one day, the larger ones weighing around 500 pounds each.

Grey wondered what angling miracles could be produced in Australian waters in a good year, if this could be taken as an example of what could be done under adverse conditions. Leaving Australia, he predicted that the country would in time "yield the most incredible and magnificent big-game fish of known and unknown species that the fishing world has ever recorded." The development of commercial fisheries in subsequent years proved that he was right.

In the record of this expedition, *An American Angler in Australia,* Grey mused upon "the humor, the sport, the thrill, the misery and ecstasy of big-game fishing."

But aside from the fishing, there was the country itself. He had spent years studying its geography and history, corresponding with native Australians and Americans who had visited its shores, but he confessed: "I was hardly prepared for this land of staggering contrasts, of unbelievable beasts, of the loveliest and strangest birds, of great modern English cities, of ranges that rivaled my beloved Arizona, and of endless forestland, or bush, as they call it, never yet adequately described, no doubt because of beauty and wildness beyond the power of any pen to delineate."

Here was another accidentally-discovered setting for a story. His Australian readers eagerly awaited the publication of *Wilderness Trek,* a novel of adventure in Australia, and all those who read it would deny Grey's statement that the beauties of the land were "beyond the power of any pen to delineate," for the pen of Zane Grey captured the rugged charm of the country, depicting it in vivid, flowing narrative sentences reminiscent of the style of James Fenimore Cooper, whose works Grey had admired since boyhood and had perhaps unconsciously imitated.

"Z.G. expeditions" had become outstanding news material, and as he sailed from port to port, the stories of his travels and his record fish were published in *The New York Times* and the *Zanesville Signal* alike. The little Ohio city that had produced Chauncey Olcott, Billie Burke, Elizabeth Robins, Hugh Wiley, Howard Chandler Christy, and the Supreme Court architect, Cass Gilbert, had not forgotten its favorite native son. Zanesvillians followed the career and works of Zane Grey with a devotion that belied the old adage that a prophet is without honor in his own country.

They had had an opportunity to honor the author back in 1921, when at the invitation of the Zanesville Rotary Club, Grey had returned to the place of his birth. He had left it as a young man with nothing but high hopes and wild dreams; he was returning as a world-renowned writer, read by millions, with a recent honorary degree in letters conferred upon him by his Alma Mater, the University of Pennsylvania, where he had graduated in dentistry years ago.

Zanesville had changed, but there were many old residents who still spoke of him as "Doc" or "Pearl." Among the young people, he was respectfully referred to as "Mr. Grey." They had read his books avidly, had seen many of the motion-picture adaptations of his novels, had read newspaper accounts of his fishing exploits, and had heard many a yarn about his boyhood pranks in The Terrace. They were excited over the declaration of Zane Grey Homecoming Week and the preparations that preceded it.

The entire town had participated in planning the event and turned out *en masse* to pay respects to the guest of honor. For weeks preceding the event, committees had been at work arranging the program. The librarian reported that not a Zane Grey novel was left on her shelves, although the library had more than one copy of every book he had ever written. Bookstores had similar reports to make as Zanesville residents swarmed in to purchase the most recent novels by the homecoming hero.

Grey had been surprised and touched by the warmth of their welcome, especially by the tremendous ovation he received from three thousand cheering youngsters who had been dismissed from school to gather in the new Weller Theatre and there hear their favorite author speak. The enthusiasm of those seated and standing in the theatre, and the disappointment of the thousand packed on the sidewalks outside the theatre, was so moving to Grey that he could scarcely find his voice. All his old shyness returned to him, and he could do little but utter the fervent hope that if any of his youthful audience had aspirations to become writers, they would seek his help without hesitation. He meant every word from the bottom of his heart, but so great was his difficulty in expressing himself that he was vastly relieved when the theatre lights dimmed and the youngsters sat back to enjoy a film adaptation of his wartime novel, *The Desert of Wheat.*

Equally touching was the large turn-out that crowded the new Masonic Temple for the civic banquet in his honor, and the Rotary Club luncheon at which he had been feted and elected to honorary membership. Their speeches and songs in his praise were sweet to his ears, but with his inborn shyness of crowds, he had longed for a brief interlude of solitude to collect his thoughts and review the memories that had come crowding into his mind as he walked down the changed but still-familiar streets.

At the first opportunity he slipped away for a quiet walk by himself, to meditate upon the changes in himself and in his native town. As he passed along Main Street, he saw many familiar faces and shook hands with people he had not seen for more than twenty years. Pausing in front of a store, he noticed a picture in the window. There was something vaguely familiar about it —a picture of a lad in a straw hat with a fishing pole over his shoulder. He glanced at the inscription beneath it and suddenly he knew. The boy was himself. With a tightening of his throat, he read the words printed beneath the old photograph:

Come along with me, Mr. Grey;
We'll go fishing at Dillon's today.
Forget Betty Zane and all the rest
For a day of sport you used to love best.

For all the honors they've paid you, I ween,
You'll gladly exchange for one glimpse of that scene.
The Plains and the Rockies bow low to your pen
But Muskingum and Licking are calling again.

There's Cannon Hill, Putnam, and Old Cedar Rock,
And the swimmin' hole down by the old steamboat
    lock,
And the diamond up at the old White House ground—
Say boy, shall I stop? How does it sound?

The verse must have been written, Grey thought, by one of his old cronies who knew all his old haunts and favorite pastimes, someone who understood the bittersweet nostalgia of this homecoming. When he had gained control of his vocal cords he stepped inside the store and inquired who had written the verse in the window. To his surprise he was introduced to a young man named Shrider who worked in the store. The youth, who had wanted to have a share in honoring his favorite author, had asked one of Zane Grey's boyhood friends for the names of their old haunts and had worked them into a poem. He was overwhelmed when the celebrated author asked him for an autographed copy of the verse.

Grey walked on, in search of the old landmarks mentioned in Shrider's poem, many of which had been lost in the rapid expansion of the city. Cannon Hill, which had been the scene of many a Fourth of July celebration, was covered with houses; McIntire Park was still there, but the portion that had once been the ball diamond was now in the midst of a residential area. He walked up the hill where the boys had coasted in the winter snow and marked the spot where Reddy Grey had been thrown from his sled and broken his arm in two places. There were many new homes on The Terrace, but Grey knew that his birthplace still remained. He remembered the number: 363 Convers Avenue.

The house was there, but the number had been changed to 705 and much of the surrounding landscape was altered. He stopped to talk to Henry Danker, who owned the house, and to reminisce upon the changes wrought by the years since Grey had played in the orchard back of the house. He could locate the exact spot where he and his fellows had dug their cave, and where his first creative effort had gone up in smoke. That had been one of the greatest tragedies of his young life, but now he could smile at it and at the boyish dreams he had put down in laborious words on rough wallpaper.

In those early dreams he had always paid homage to a blue-eyed blonde, beautiful, cool, and remote. He smiled to think of the contrasting reality. Dolly Grey, with her wavy brown hair, her plump comfortable figure, her laughing eyes, and her warm friendly smile, was quite unlike the dream girl, but she had made his life much more than he had ever dared hope it would be. And in the meantime, the blue-eyed blonde girl—who doubtless had been unaware of the schoolboy adulation she inspired—was happily married and had a daughter of her own, a girl slightly older than Romer Grey.

It was through a curious turn of fate that Grey had

met the girl, Louise, who bore such a striking resemblance to her mother that it recalled all his youthful daydreams and made him startlingly aware that the blonde vision of his schoolboy days was still very much alive in his mind. She had been so much a part of his fantasies that he had been unaware of her existence there until the moment he was confronted by her real-life image. It was at the banquet in the large ballroom of the Masonic Temple. He had leaned back in his chair, turning his eyes briefly away from the stage while the master of ceremonies announced the next feature of the program, ". . . a dramatic interpretation of the poem, *Gold*, written by another talented Zanesville native, Sister Monica, of the Brown County Convent."

Applause, and then there appeared before him the flaxen-haired, blue-eyed vision. He had not caught her name, but he knew who she was. The likeness was unmistakable. And with sudden, startling clarity he saw that this was the girl who had played the role of heroine in so many of his Western romances. In his real life, she had ceased to exist long ago; but in his creative facet she was ever present, and he had long been disappointed that in all the movies that had been based on his novels, no actress had been found who fit his mental picture of the heroine. He had had to go back to Zanesville, back to his boyhood, to find her.

The Last Great Adventure

Zane Grey lived to see many of his dreams come true, and he died while life was still a glorious adventure. In 1937, after his visit to Australia, he wrote: "It seems, as the years go by, that every camp I pitch in places far from home grows more beautiful and romantic." He had never wearied of traveling, and it was with all the zest of youth that he set out in 1938 to circle the globe and thus to fulfill one more life-long dream. When he returned to Altadena in the autumn of 1939 it was to face the last great adventure.

Physicians told him he had coronary thrombosis, a disease of the heart which could not be cured. They warned him against over-exertion, regardless of his own private theory that a rugged outdoor life is the best treatment for bodily ills. He submitted to treatment but went about his work in much the same way, spending several days autographing copies of *Western Union*, his latest historical novel, just off the press. He was in excellent spirits and certainly gave no indication of being a sick man.

Death came swiftly. Grey went to bed one night

complaining of what he termed "a slight case of indigestion." Next morning he arose at the usual hour, suffered a sudden heart attack, and never regained consciousness. Dolly Grey was at his side when he died.

While the Grey family gathered for quiet private services at a Pasadena funeral home prior to cremation of Zane Grey's mortal remains, as he himself had requested, people everywhere were reading and hearing of his life and death. A world that had not yet recovered from the first shock of the outbreak of war in Europe was saddened by the news that flashed from San Francisco to New York, from Nova Scotia to Vancouver, from London to Sydney, to every country the author had visited and to those where he was known only through his translated books.

"Zane Grey is dead."

The news was repeated among ranchers and cowhands in Arizona, prospectors in Oregon, boatmen in Mexico, anglers in Florida, sportsmen all over the world and readers in all walks of life. Australian headlines told of it, and in New Zealand Maori tribesmen who read of it recalled the meeting at which they had conferred upon Zane Grey the honorary title of *Maui*, after the greatest of Maori fishermen. The news reached the ears of native Tahitians and inhabitants of little Mexican villages where he was remembered for his friendliness, his quiet dignity and courtesy. In London it was a front-page story; even the *Daily Mail*, whose first page had been devoted exclusively to war news for weeks, carried a portrait of Zane Grey and an obituary notice.

New York newspapers were filled with little human interest stories and personal reminiscences of "people who knew him when." One of these was Robert H. (Bob) Davis, former editor of *Munsey's Magazine*, famed as a confidante of writers, and at the time of Grey's death, serving as roving correspondent for the *New York Sun*. Davis had often spoken derisively of his friend's fish stories, remarking that "If Zane went out with a mosquito net to catch minnows, he could make it sound like a Roman gladiator setting forth to slay whales in the Tiber." Another time, on reading Grey's statement to the effect that a battle with a hard-fighting tuna "liberates the brute instinct in man," the irrepressible Davis quipped, "It also liberates the qualities of a liar."

It was all good-natured banter, for the two had been the best of friends ever since the days when Davis gave Grey the first real encouragement ever offered him by a professional in the writing field. It was in appreciation of Davis' encouraging words that Grey had long ago written Davis a letter with instructions on the envelope to open it only when he was "quite ill or feeling blue." The years had rolled by and on that October day in 1939, the envelope, yellowed with age, still remained unopened. But Davis' secretary surmised that when he returned from his overseas assignment, he would be feeling sufficiently blue over the death of his friend to open the letter.

The New York "House of Harper," publishers of Zane Grey books for nearly thirty years, received the news of his death even as his latest book, *Western Union*, was going on sale. They predicted it would be even more successful than many of his earlier books, dealing as it did with the glamorous story of the creation and development of the early telegraph system through hostile Indian territory in the West. Bookstores were placing large orders and movie producers were already making fabulous offers for the script. There were three more

Zane Grey manuscripts left to be revised by Mrs. Grey and published posthumously: *The Frontier Wife, The Young George Washington,* and *30,000 on the Hoof.* In addition to these manuscripts, there was in his study the manuscript of a four-act play which the versatile author had written, unknown to his publishers or even to members of his own family.

At the offices of Grosset and Dunlap, the New York publishing house that had been reprinting Zane Grey novels for more than twenty years, during which time they had sold thirteen million copies, there were many recollections of the famous author and of another Zanesville native, recently deceased, who had been instrumental in making the Zane Grey romances best-sellers. Sam Jenkins, who had started his career as a newsboy in Zanesville and later graduated to the ownership of a bookstore, left Ohio at the turn of the century and went to New York. There he joined the firm of Grosset and Dunlap, then in its infancy, as a book agent, and traveled all over the country merchandising the popular reprints of current literature. He had taken great pleasure and pride in boosting the sales on Zane Grey novels, for he still entertained memories of the author as a lad in Zanesville, haunting the Jenkins newsstand to steal glimpses into the dime novels on the shelf.

To Zanesville, Ohio, the news came as a great shock. There were many who remembered him from boyhood days and many who had come to know him since his memorable homecoming in 1921. Among these was a young woman, to whom the passing of Zane Grey meant the loss of a great friend and benefactor.

"I was only fourteen when I first met Mr. Grey," she recalled, "although of course I had heard my parents speak of him many times. I was on the program arranged for his homecoming. I read a poem written by one of the sisters at the convent I was attending, and Mr. Grey was so pleased with it that he asked me to come to California to study literature and interpretive drama under his supervision. My parents consented, and I spent a wonderful six months with the Grey family at Altadena. Mrs. Grey took me in just like a member of the family, and Mr. Grey was very kind to me too. I didn't kill myself studying; there was always time for tennis or horseback riding. They had even bought a horse especially for me during my first visit there. I went again the next summer and continued studying, but I'm afraid Mr. Grey overrated my so-called talent. He had hopes of a movie career for me, but I just didn't make the grade. I was sorry to disappoint him and to come back to Zanesville to admit my failure, but I always kept in touch with the Grey family and they stopped in to visit whenever they passed through on the way to New York. Mr. Grey always believed that Hollywood was wrong and he was right—but I was convinced that I wasn't movie material, even though I appreciated everything he did for me."

Among the older residents of Zanesville was Sam Playford, a former schoolmate of Zane Grey and a retired mail carrier. "Zane Grey dead?" he repeated, when he heard the news. "Why, I knew him when we were kids. We went to school together. I met him again in California only a couple of years ago and we talked over old times." Playford reminisced about the old schooldays when he and Zane Grey had played baseball on opposing teams, and of the day many years later when he was wintering in California and called at the Grey home in Altadena to renew old acquaintances.

"He lived in a huge house," Playford recalled. "I went

up a long walk and knocked on the door. Zane—or Pearl, as I knew him—answered the door himself.

"I said, 'Hello, Pearl.'

"He looked at me, puzzled, and said, 'I'm afraid you've got one on me.'

" 'I'm Sam Playford, of Zanesville,' I said.

" 'Come in,' he said heartily. 'Let's talk over the old baseball games we played back there in Ohio.'

"He took me through a big room filled with sea shells and on back to his study. We spent the whole afternoon there, recalling the old days at Zanesville, talking mostly about athletics. He had the same self-assurance then as he had fifty years ago, when I first knew him. Always on the go. Always trying to keep young. Why, he was more than sixty years old then and still playing tennis with his children, and making them hump on the courts, too. . . .

"And now he's dead. Well, even though he was six years younger than I, and never wanted to grow old, I suppose it had to come sometime."

Playford described Grey as "self-confident and cocky, both as a boy and as a man," an impression which was not shared by those who had known him intimately through the years. He may have given that appearance; but what Playford interpreted as "cockiness" was actually a fixed determination to accomplish whatever he set out to do. He had never made an active campaign, as Playford imagined, "to stay young." He lived an active life to the last because it was the only way he knew how to live, the only way he would have wanted to live even if he had known that it would shorten his life, as it probably did.

People of Zanesville discussed a movement to erect a memorial to Zane Grey, and Henry Danker, who owned the author's birthplace on Convers Avenue, offered it to the Ohio Archaeological and Historical Society to be used as a historical museum memorializing the city's celebrated son, if the movement carried through. To date the plan has not been carried out, but Zanesville has not forgotten. Every year countless tourists, crossing the famous Y bridge into the heart of Zanesville, are directed to the author's birthplace; many of them pass by the Scout camp that bears his name, or dine in the Zane Grey Room of the city's largest hotel.

One of the most fitting memorials is the liberty ship, *Zane Grey*, launched during the darkest days of the Second World War. In the impressive dedication ceremony, Mrs. Zane Grey was the sponsor and acting as maid of honor was Mrs. Robert W. Carney—the former Betty Zane Grey. Her husband, then on active duty as a lieutenant in the Army Air Force, was unable to attend, but their two daughters, Michele and Carol, were present. Lt. (j.g.) Loren Grey, home on furlough for the first time during his fifteen months of service in the Pacific theatre, was granted an extension of time so that he could be on hand, and Romer Grey left his ranching duties long enough to attend the ceremony.

There had been a time when Zane Grey expected, and perhaps hoped, that his eldest son would carry on in his footsteps, for the boy showed great verbal facility even at an early age. But even as his famous father had turned away from dentistry, Romer abandoned any thought he might have entertained of becoming a writer. He preferred the life of a rancher, keeping in touch with the literary world only as an editorial adviser on *Zane Grey's Western Magazine*, a monthly publication of authentic Western fiction, featuring in each issue an adaptation of one of Zane Grey's incomparable romances of the Old West.

The wide circulation of the magazine, the continued sale of Zane Grey books, many of which have been published since his death, and the crowds that flock to the theatres where Zane Grey films are showing, all bear evidence of the permanent appeal of Zane Grey among writers of American fiction. No one has ever been able to imitate him; no one would ever try to replace him.

The Books of Zane Grey

NOVELS

Betty Zane (Charles Francis Press, 1903). Reprinted by
  Grosset & Dunlap.

    Zane Grey's first book, a historical novel relating
the exploits of his own ancestors, the pioneer Zanes,
and the heroism of Betty Zane in saving the besieged
Fort Henry.

The Spirit of the Border (A. L. Burt Co., 1906). Reprinted by Grosset & Dunlap.

    A sequel to *Betty Zane,* this story portrays the
Ohio frontier as a wild and forbidding place, where
the only law was a long rifle and a man lived only
as long as he could shoot faster and straighter than
his enemies.

The Last Trail (A. L. Burt Co., 1909). Reprinted by
  Grosset & Dunlap.

    Third in the series of frontier historical novels,
this follows the adventures of the Indian scout,
Jonathan Zane, brother of Betty Zane and a friend
of Lew Wetzel, the Avenger, whose deadly rifle
earned him the title "Wind of Death," the only
name by which the Indians knew him.

The Heritage of the Desert (Harper & Brothers, 1910).
  Reprinted by Grosset & Dunlap.

    The girl Mescal, half-Indian and half-Spanish,
escapes from a Mormon colony to avoid a hated
marriage and meets a young Easterner who has come

to Arizona for his health. Their love story is unfolded against the background of the colorful desert land with which the author was so familiar.

Riders of the Purple Sage (Harper & Brothers, 1912). Reprinted by Grosset & Dunlap.

The never - to - be - forgotten romance which brought fame to Zane Grey after years of struggling for recognition. Grey's vivid descriptions of the sagebrush country have never been equaled. His characters are real people and the magnificent horses, Black Star and Night, are real horses, described as only a lover of fine horses could describe them.

Desert Gold (Harper & Brothers, 1913). Reprinted by Grosset & Dunlap.

In the mysterious desert, near the Mexican border, a girl finds the grave of her father and the gold mine he had discovered and, dying of heat and thirst, had willed to her. The Grosset & Dunlap reprint is illustrated by scenes from the photoplay produced by Zane Grey's own company.

The Light of Western Stars (Harper & Brothers, 1914). Reprinted by Grosset & Dunlap.

The story of a New York society girl who buys a ranch in New Mexico and finds herself involved in frontier warfare and a love affair with one of the dashing cowboys she had feared before she knew the ways of the West.

The Lone Star Ranger (Harper & Brothers, 1915). Reprinted by Grosset & Dunlap.

The Texas border in the early Seventies provides the background for this romance of a man, hunted by outlaws and honest men alike, who is brought back to civilization by the Texas Rangers and given his second chance.

The Rainbow Trail (Harper & Brothers, 1915). Reprinted by Grosset & Dunlap.

A young minister, at odds with his flock, is convinced of his failure and becomes a wanderer in the lonely Western uplands, where he finds new faith and love. This novel appeared serially under the title *The Desert Crucible*.

The Border Legion (Harper & Brothers, 1916). Reprinted by Grosset & Dunlap.

A romance of the southern Idaho border in the days of the California gold rush, and of the impact of sudden wealth—or the prospect of it—upon men and women, good and bad.

Wildfire (Harper & Brothers, 1916). Reprinted by Grosset & Dunlap.

In this thrilling story a young man captures the beautiful red stallion, Wildfire, but it remains for a courageous girl to tame the wild horse—and win the heart of its rider. The Grosset & Dunlap edition is illustrated by scenes from the photoplay, a Goldwyn production.

The U.P. Trail (Harper & Brothers, 1918). Reprinted by Grosset & Dunlap.

Here is an epic of a mighty episode in the history of this country, with its climax in the completion of the Union Pacific railroad as a monument to heroic struggle and human perseverance. This book was published also as "The Roaring U.P. Trail."

The Desert of Wheat (Harper & Brothers, 1919). Reprinted by Grosset & Dunlap.

This story, despite its World War background, breathes the spirit of the Old West when men took the law into their own hands—in this case to prevent enemy aliens from destroying the great wheat fields of Golden Valley.

The Man of the Forest (Harper & Brothers, 1920). Reprinted by Grosset & Dunlap.

Milt Dale was happy in the quiet solitude of the mountain forest, until two girls from the East appeared on the scene, and he was forced to share his woodland home with them as a refuge from the outlaws who were plotting against their lives and property. He resented their intrusion—until they were gone and he found the forest too empty for him.

The Mysterious Rider (Harper & Brothers, 1921). Reprinted by Grosset & Dunlap.

No one knew where the mysterious rider came from or what his past had been, but they knew that he was a man of strong loves and hates, quick with a gun and slow to forget an injustice. Only his violent, tragic death revealed the secret of his past.

To the Last Man (Harper & Brothers, 1922). Reprinted by Grosset & Dunlap.

The stirring story of a feud waged between two unforgiving factions who only realized its utter futility when it was too late.

Wanderer of the Wasteland (Harper & Brothers, 1923). Reprinted by Grosset & Dunlap.

The story of a man who takes refuge in the Great American desert in his attempt to escape the law and memories of his dark past. This book bears the inscription: "Dedicated to my wife, Lina Elise Grey, without whose love, faith, spirit and help I never could have written this novel."

The Call of the Canyon (Harper & Brothers, 1924). Reprinted by Grosset & Dunlap.

A New York society girl goes to Arizona to visit

her fiance, who has been sent there for his health, and despite her original fears of this primitive country, she finds that she can never again adjust to her old meaningless existence in the East.

The Vanishing American (Harper & Brothers, 1925). Reprinted by Grosset & Dunlap.

This is the great romance of the American Indian —revealing in the swift march of its events the tragedy and glory of a whole race, and the true essence of the West, as only Zane Grey could express it.

The Thundering Herd (Harper & Brothers, 1925). Reprinted by Grosset & Dunlap.

This is an unsurpassed picture of the Old West— miles of great prairie covered by buffalo herds; reckless hard-riding plainsmen, buffalo hunters, Indians, bandits—the whole epoch of the Western pioneer, centering on the destruction of the thundering herds of buffalo.

Under the Tonto Rim (Harper & Brothers, 1926). Reprinted by Grosset & Dunlap.

A young woman leaves home and goes into the backwoods country of the Arizona Tonto Rim as a social worker. She plays a colorful role in the fascinating community and finds happiness in the love of one of its native sons. This story was published serially by the Curtis Publishing Company under the title, *The Bee Hunter*.

Forlorn River (Harper & Brothers, 1927). Reprinted by Grosset & Dunlap.

This is a story of the lawless days of cattle thieves and the thrilling pursuit and capture of wild horses. It is full of the intensity and dash which made up life then and which Zane Grey alone has been able to bring to life in print.

Valley of Wild Horses (Harper & Brothers, 1927). Reprinted by Grosset & Dunlap.

Young Panhandle Smith grows to manhood in the open range of the Southwest and seeks his fortune in a rock-rimmed canyon where hundreds of glorious, stampeding wild horses represent the prize of a lifetime.

Stairs of Sand (Harper & Brothers, 1928). Reprinted by Grosset & Dunlap.

The scene of this story is laid in the desert of Southern California, where men fight and kill for precious waterhole rights.

"Nevada" (Harper & Brothers, 1928). Reprinted by Grosset & Dunlap.

That was the only name by which the girl knew him; she would never have guessed that his reputation as a gunman ranked second only to Billy the Kid.

Wild Horse Mesa (Harper & Brothers, 1928). Reprinted by Grosset & Dunlap.

A resolute party sets forth to conquer Wild Horse Mesa and to capture the phantom stallion, Panguitch. A girl accompanies her father on the hunt and participates in the thrilling capture, witnessing Panguitch's last stand.

Fighting Caravans (Harper & Brothers, 1929). Reprinted by Grosset & Dunlap.

Two young people, a boy and a girl, are orphaned by an Indian raid upon a caravan of freighters trekking across hostile territory, become separated and are lost in the vastness of the great frontier.

The Shepherd of Guadaloupe (Harper & Brothers, 1930). Reprinted by Grosset & Dunlap.

A young man returns from the War to fight for

his life, his lost health, and his father's ranch, which had fallen to the hands of his unscrupulous business enemies.

Raiders of Spanish Peaks (Harper & Brothers, 1931). Reprinted by Grosset & Dunlap.

Spanish Peaks Ranch was an abandoned United States military post, bought by an Eastern family who found that warfare continued there—between ranchers and rustlers.

Sunset Pass (Harper & Brothers, 1931). Reprinted by Grosset & Dunlap.

A daring young rider returns to his native town of Wagontongue and goes to work for the clan that reigns supreme in the valley beyond Sunset Pass. There is something sinister in the air of that locked-in valley, and the peril that awaits the daughter of the clan is discovered almost too late.

West of the Pecos (Harper & Brothers, 1931). Reprinted by Grosset & Dunlap.

This is the story of days when there was reputedly "no law west of the River Pecos," of the mysterious Pecos Smith and his ride to rescue Rill from the men who had murdered her father. Richard Dix starred in the motion picture version.

The Lost Wagon Train (Harper & Brothers, 1932). Reprinted by Grosset & Dunlap.

In the days following the Civil War, a train of 160 wagons headed West and disappeared from sight. The sole survivor of the horrible Indian massacre is a little girl. Twenty years later she is reunited with her father who had turned brigand and joined with an Indian tribe in raids against his own people.

Arizona Ames (Harper & Brothers, 1932). Reprinted by Grosset & Dunlap.

Arizona Ames was a bad man, quick as lightning with a six-shooter, and with many notches in his gun. But he believed in justice, even if it had to be enforced beyond the reach of the law.

Robbers' Roost (Harper & Brothers, 1932). Reprinted by Grosset & Dunlap.

In the roaring Seventies, deep in the picturesque fastnesses of Utah, this drama unfolds in a tensely gripping narrative of the battle that took place in Robbers' Roost between rival outlaw gangs.

The Drift Fence (Harper & Brothers, 1932). Reprinted by Grosset & Dunlap.

The drift fence was built by a wealthy cattle rancher across the fertile valley which was rightfully open to anyone's cattle. Even in the peaceful Pleasant Valley country, disputes over water rights meant gunplay, and the fence became the center of warfare.

The Hash Knife Outfit (Harper & Brothers, 1933). Reprinted by Grosset & Dunlap.

The serial version of this story, published in *Collier's Weekly*, appeared under the title, *The Yellow Jacket Feud*. This is a sequel to *The Drift Fence*, carrying on the feud between the Diamond ranchhands and the lawless Hash Knife Outfit.

Code of the West (Harper & Brothers, 1934). Reprinted by Grosset & Dunlap.

When flirtatious Georgiana came to the Tonto Basin from the East, she had heard neither of chivalry nor of loyalty, but when the trouble started she learned about the code of the West.

Thunder Mountain (Harper & Brothers, 1935). Reprinted by Grosset & Dunlap.

Three brothers, prospecting in northern Idaho, prove that the dying Indian had spoken the truth when he said that there was gold in Thunder Mountain—even nuggets lying above the ground. The gold rush that followed the discovery brought treachery and terror to the little mountain town.

Knights of the Range (Harper & Brothers, 1936). Reprinted by Grosset & Dunlap.

Holly Ripple, who has lived a sheltered life at Eastern boarding schools, finds herself sole owner of the Don Carlos Rancho. She is forced to organize a vigilante outfit of her own to protect her fifty thousand head of cattle from rustlers.

The Trail Driver (Harper & Brothers, 1936). Reprinted by Grosset & Dunlap.

This is a thrilling story of treacherous Indians, cattle-rustlers, stampedes, and finally that great cattle drive of 1871 when over four thousand longhorns were driven from San Antonio to Dodge City, Kansas. The historic American scene is portrayed vigorously and graphically by the writer who knew every foot of the territory of which he wrote.

Majesty's Rancho (Harper & Brothers, 1937). Reprinted by Grosset & Dunlap.

A modern sequel to *The Light of Western Stars*, in which the daughter of Majesty Hammond and Gene Stewart is kidnaped by the rustlers who have been raiding the Arizona ranch, and Lance Sidway comes to the rescue with his beautiful horse, whose name, Umpqua, the Indian word for "swift," proves most appropriate.

Western Union (Harper & Brothers, 1939). Reprinted by Grosset & Dunlap.

This historical novel, based on the hardships and adventures incident to the establishment of telegraph communication in the West, is dedicated "To a single strand of iron wire." Darryl Zanuck produced the motion picture version.

30,000 on the Hoof (Harper & Brothers, 1940). Reprinted by Grosset & Dunlap.

The saga of a man and woman who undertake the tremendous task of carving a home for themselves and their future family from the wilderness of Arizona, and realize their dream of raising on their homestead ranch a large herd of cattle.

Twin Sombreros (Harper & Brothers, 1940). Reprinted by Grosset & Dunlap.

A story of murder and revenge, merciless rustlers and hard-riding cowhands, full of fast action and a romance to touch the heart.

Wilderness Trek (Harper & Brothers, 1944). Reprinted by Grosset & Dunlap.

A novel with an Australian setting, narrating the adventures of two American cowboys who sailed to this far-off land and hired themselves out to help drive a herd of cattle to the Kimberleys through bush country as wild and strange to them as to the readers.

Shadow on the Trail (Harper & Brothers, 1946). Reprinted by Grosset & Dunlap.

In the days of the frontier West, it was not unusual for desperadoes and fugitives from justice to disappear from the face of the earth, never to be heard of again. This is the story of one who disappeared, and returned to re-establish himself in a law-abiding society.

Rogue River Feud (Harper & Brothers, 1948).

This story was published serially under the title, *Rustlers of Silver River*. It tells of the feud among market fishermen in the Rogue River country of Oregon, where the author spent many months fishing and exploring the length of the river.

BOOKS FOR BOYS

The Last of the Plainsmen (The Outing Publishing Co., 1908). Reprinted by Grosset & Dunlap.

This is the true story of the author's first expedition into the great West, in the company of Buffalo Jones, "the last of the plainsmen."

The Shortstop (A. C. McClurg & Co., 1909). Reprinted by Grosset & Dunlap.

A story of professional baseball, and the luck that makes or breaks a newcomer to the game.

The Young Forester (Harper & Brothers, 1910). Reprinted by Grosset & Dunlap.

This book, the first in the Ken Ward series, relates the adventures of a young Eastern lad who goes West to spend his summer vacation with a forest ranger friend in Arizona. Bear hunts, fishing trips, a forest fire, and a big lumber steal add up to make an exciting summer.

The Young Pitcher (Harper & Brothers, 1911). Reprinted by Grosset & Dunlap.

This exciting story of Ken Ward's baseball career at Wayne College, where he is studying forestry, is a favorite with all boys who love "the great American game."

The Young Lion Hunter (Harper & Brothers, 1911). Reprinted by Grosset & Dunlap.

Ken Ward and his brother, Hal, spend the summer on a forest preserve in Utah and join the government rangers in a hunt to rid the preserve of the fierce and dangerous lions.

Ken Ward in the Jungle (Harper & Brothers, 1912). Reprinted by Grosset & Dunlap.

Ken Ward goes on a field trip into the wilds of Mexican jungles with his brother, Hal, and follows an uncharted jungle river to its source in an expedition filled with humor and terror.

The Redheaded Outfield and Other Baseball Stories (McClure Newspaper Syndicate, 1915). Reprinted by Grosset & Dunlap.

This is a collection of topnotch baseball stories, beginning with "The Redheaded Outfield" in which three crazy redheads provide headaches for their manager, laughs for their teammates, and thrills for the bleachers.

Roping Lions in the Grand Canyon (Harper & Brothers, 1922). Reprinted by Grosset & Dunlap.

This is the true and thrilling story of the author's experiences with Buffalo Jones in the Grand Canyon, capturing lions alive. In a brief foreword the author expresses the hope that the book will generate in his young readers "the impulse which may help to preserve our great outdoors for future generations."

Tappan's Burro and Other Stories (Harper & Brothers, 1923). Reprinted by Grosset & Dunlap.

Here is a collection of five short stories, all of them laid in remote and picturesque places known to few people other than Zane Grey, and all of them packed with adventure. The title story is of the prospector, Tappan, who would certainly have lost his life in Death Valley but for his faithful little burro.

Don, the Story of a Lion Dog (Harper & Brothers, 1928). Illustrated by Kurt Wiese.

The touching story of a noble dog who participated in the Grand Canyon lion hunt with Grey and Buffalo Jones. He hated men—but Grey had saved his life, and when the occasion arose, Don returned the favor.

The Wolf-Tracker (Harper & Brothers, 1930). Illustrated by Kurt Wiese.

"Old Gray" was a lone wolf with a history of many cattle-killings behind him. A $5000 reward was offered for his pelt, but the stranger who called himself "The Tracker" came to Arizona not for money but to rid the range of the elusive killer.

Zane Grey's Book of Camps and Trails (Harper & Brothers, 1931).

The story of Romer Grey's first trip into the Arizona wilderness with his father, at the age of nine.

King of the Royal Mounted and Ghost Guns of Roaring River (Racine, Wisconsin: Whitman Publishing Co., 1946).

Based on the famous newspaper strip by Zane Grey.

OUTDOOR BOOKS

Tales of Fishes (Harper & Brothers, 1919), with illustrations from photographs by the author.

Fish stories from the author's experiences in Mexico, the Gulf Stream, and off Catalina Island, with interesting notes from his diary.

Tales of Lonely Trails (Harper & Brothers, 1922), with photographic illustrations.

This collection contains accounts of Zane Grey's expedition to Nonnezoshe, the Rainbow Bridge, hunting trips in Colorado and the Tonto Basin of Arizona, his trek across Death Valley, and his adventures in Grand Canyon roping live lions.

Tales of Southern Rivers (Harper & Brothers, 1924), with photographic illustrations.

Here are narratives of Zane Grey's experiences in deep-sea fishing in the Gulf of Mexico and freshwater fishing in the rivers and lagoons of the Florida Everglades, topped off with an account of an exploratory trip "Down an Unknown Jungle River" in Mexico.

Tales of Fishing Virgin Seas (Harper & Brothers, 1925), with photographic illustrations.

The account of Zane Grey's expedition to the South Sea Islands in 1924, handsomely illustrated with sketches by Lillian Wilhelm Smith and striking photographs by the author and members of his party.

Tales of the Angler's Eldorado, New Zealand (Harper & Brothers, 1926), with more than a hundred photographs by Zane Grey and drawings by Frank E. Phares.

The waters surrounding New Zealand were alive with fish of many varieties, and Grey returned again and again, encouraged by the marvelous luck of his first expedition.

Tales of Swordfish and Tuna (Harper & Brothers, 1927), with photographic illustrations by the author and drawings by Frank E. Phares.

This book is dedicated "to my brother, R.C., in memory of the old Zanesville boyhood days that made us fishermen." It begins with tales of tuna fishing at Avalon and Nova Scotia and ends with Loren Grey's first fish story, written at the age of ten, when he landed a barracuda that was "very fast but not so specticculer."

Tales of Fresh-Water Fishing (Harper & Brothers, 1928), with 100 illustrations from photographs by the author.

Here are narratives of Zane Grey's fishing experiences, man and boy, in the streams of Pennsylvania, Ohio, New York, Washington, and Oregon.

Tales of Tahitian Waters (Harper & Brothers, 1931), with many photographic illustrations.

In this handsomely illustrated volume the author tells of three fishing seasons at Tahiti where he caught world-record dolphin and marlin and two new species of fish which he named the Silver Marlin and the Great Tahitian Striped Marlin. He collected many specimens which were presented to aquariums and to the Museum of Natural History in New York City.

An American Angler in Australia (Harper & Brothers, 1937), with illustrations from photographs by the author and members of his party.

A chronicle of the author's adventures in Australian waters, including photographs of his world-record catches of tiger shark and marlin and breathtaking play-by-play descriptions of how these record fish were landed.

Produced under the editorial supervision of
ELLIOTT W. McDOWELL
Designed by FAY TRAVERS
Manufactured by H. WOLFF BOOK MFG. CO., INC.